Table of Contents

Introduction

Chapter 1: My Mission

Chapter 2: What is Emotional Immaturity?

Chapter 3: Different Types of Emotionally Immature Parents

Chapter 4: The Consequences of Growing Up with Emotionally Immature Parents

Chapter 5: Common "If" Thoughts and How to Change Them Trough Self-love

Chapter 6: Four Steps to Inner-Healing

Chapter 7: How to Practice Self-care and Unlock Your Potential

Chapter 8: How to Heal the Relationships with Your Parents

Chapter 9: How to Let Go of a Toxic Relationship

Chapter 10: How to Overcome the Effects of Your Upbringing and Become a Good Parent to Your Own Children

Chapter 11: Don't Give Up

Conclusion

Sources

INTRODUCTION

World-renowned psychologist Sigmund Freud once said, "There is no greater need in childhood than to feel the protection of parents." This wasn't just his opinion or a passing fancy. Instead, it was the conclusion he came to after spending years studying the causes of the psychological conditions that plagued countless people in his time. Freud discovered that one of the main common denominators among people struggling with psychological trauma was an unhealthy childhood. Unfortunately, the same traumas and issues continue to plague growing numbers of people in modern times. Equally tragic, most of these issues can still be traced to an unhealthy childhood. In fact, it is estimated that as many as one in four people suffers from the trauma of having at least one toxic parent in their life.

Fortunately, no matter how traumatic or toxic your childhood might have been, you can still live a life that is full of love, meaning, and happiness. The key is to recognize the influences that your past is having on your current day-to-day life. You might be living a life of solitude, afraid that people will reject you for not being good enough. Or you might be stuck in a toxic relationship, one that resembles the relationship you had with your parents while growing up. Perhaps you are filled with rage, unleashing your anger at the slightest of triggers and bringing misery to your own family. Even worse, maybe you are afraid to have a family of your own in case you turn out to be just like your parents. No matter what issues you face as an adult the bottom line is that you can be cured of the pain and scars of your past, and thus become a better person, spouse, and parent in the here and now.

This book will provide a wide range of insights that will enable you to heal the wounds of a toxic relationship in your own life. It will first reveal the signs that you are or have been in a toxic relationship. It will discuss the various types of emotionally immature parents and the different impacts they can have on a person's emotional and mental wellbeing. Next, you will be guided through the process of eliminating self-doubt and the need to find happiness in material acquisition or social prestige. Only by freeing yourself of such damaging behavior can you begin to engage in the practices that will lead to self-healing and the creation of a happy and fulfilling life.

The next step is to begin the process of self-healing itself. This book will explore numerous different techniques proven to help any person recover from a traumatic past and discover the happiness and wellbeing they truly deserve. These techniques cover a wide range, including such things as yoga, meditation, art therapy, and several other proven methods of recovery. No matter your lifestyle, there will be several self-healing techniques that will be right for you. Finally, this book will help you to address your relationship with your emotionally immature parents. A whole chapter is devoted to the process of creating a healthy and mutually beneficial relationship with them, thereby allowing you to live your life without having to totally cut yourself away from your past. However, in the event that such a reconciliation is beyond reach, there is a chapter devoted to coping with the painful choice of having to sever ties with your parents in order to move on with your life.

By the time you finish reading this book, you will have all the tools you need to create the life of your dreams. Whether you want to just be a better person in general, with greater self-confidence and ambition, or you want to be a better person in terms of your relationships with others— being a better friend, spouse or parent, this book will help you achieve your goal. Best of all, when you finish reading this book, you will be able to share your knowledge with others who face the same struggles due to their own toxic relationships. Thus, in addition to healing your own wounds and getting your life back on track, you can help others do the same. Once you help another person find happiness in their life, you will discover that the only thing better than breaking free of your own toxic past is helping others to break free from theirs!

WAIT !!!
READ THIS BEFORE GOING ANY FURTHER!

How would you like to get your next eBook **FREE** <u>and</u> get new books for **FREE** too before they are publicly released?

Join our Self Empowerment Team today and receive your next (and future) books for **FREE**! Signing up is easy and completely free!!

Check out this page for more info!

www.SelfEmpowermentTeam.com/SignUp

As A Token of My Gratitude...

I'd like to offer you this amazing resource which my clients pay for. It is a report I written when I first began my journey.

Click on the picture above or navigate to the website below to join my exclusive email list. Upon joining, you will receive this incredible report on how to recognize an abusive relationship.

If you ask most people on the street what an abusive relationship is, chances are you'd get a description of physical abuse. And yes, that is most certainly an abusive relationship. However, abuse comes in many forms. The actual meaning of abuse is when someone exerts control over another person.

Find out more about recognizing an abusive relationship and learn how to take control over your life by clicking on the book above or by going to this link:

http://bit.ly/RecognizeAbusiveRelationship

CHAPTER 1

My Mission

Whenever you see a book about a topic as complex as emotionally immature parents, one of the first things you wonder is what makes the author qualified to write a book on the subject. Many authors have backgrounds in higher education, earning degrees in such fields as psychology and behavioral studies. While there is a lot to be said about the lessons such an education can provide, there is also a lot to be said about the lessons gained through personal experience. That is where my credentials begin. I am the product of emotionally immature parents, and I suffered an emotionally toxic and traumatic childhood, one that affected my life for many years to come. I fell into a behavioral pattern that led to many mistakes and regrets until I finally discovered the crux of the issue. Only then was I able to make the changes necessary to fix my life. The lessons I learned along the way are the insights I share in this book. However, before reading those insights, it is important that you know the journey that led me to their discovery. This is my story:

I was an ordinary child, growing up in an ordinary home. Or at least that's what I believed. As a child, you never really know what your experiences aren't as normal as they should be. The truth was that my mother was one of those people who had never been satisfied with her life. As a result, she tried to use my life to fulfill her dreams. She made me pursue things she enjoyed, and she would always compare me to her dream-self. Needless to say, I was never able to live up to those standards, and thus was a constant disappointment to her.

Alternatively, my father was a bit more distant. He was the one who worked a full-time job in order to pay the bills. Therefore he wasn't home during the day, and so I usually didn't see him until dinner time. Unfortunately, he was unable to cope with the stresses of day-to-day life, and so he could be easily triggered by even the smallest of events. A spilled drink, cold food, or the simplest of statements could send him into a rage. As a child, I became accustomed to living a life where I felt as though I was constantly walking on eggshells, knowing that I would eventually make a wrong step and awaken the monster within my father. Yet I believed that this was normal.

As I made friends and experienced other people's family dynamics, I realized that my home life was in fact, far from normal. Unfortunately, this only made things worse for me. The simple truth was that I blamed myself for the misery that my parents suffered. Whether this was due to my mother constantly telling me I wasn't good enough, or whether it was because of the anger my father unleashed on me, I don't know. Perhaps I was just a child trying to make sense of things, and I decided that I was to blame for everyone else's unhappiness. In any event, I truly did believe that I was the reason why my parents were so unhappy with life.

This resulted in me retreating into myself as I grew up. In school, I had almost no real friends, and I did my best to fly under the proverbial radar. I was convinced that I would never live up to anyone's standards, and so I just wanted to be ignored. Eventually, I found a way to focus my energies on my studies. Whether it was in an attempt to please my mother or it was simply a way to find purpose in my life I became an overly ambitious student, one who was eager to be the best in every way possible. Even so, I never sought recognition or reward. I just needed to prove to myself that I was capable of being good at something.

By the time I graduated high school, I was beginning to feel the burden of spending my life living up to other people's expectations. I decided to enroll in a college that was far from home, one where I could finally escape the shadow of my parents and start to become my own person. The taste of freedom was intoxicating, and the experiences that college life provided was everything I could have imagined. In fact, it was beyond my wildest dreams!

That was especially true when I found myself falling head over heels in love with a guy I met in my freshman year. It was truly a case of love at first sight. He listened to me in a way no one else had ever done, and I became addicted to the attention he paid me. Needless to say, when he proposed after only four months, I said "Yes" and promptly moved in with him. This, I thought, was the beginning of a better life; one far away from the toxic nature of my parents, one that would be full of love, happiness and everything else I never had as a child.

Two months later, I was pregnant. This prompted us to get married without any further delay and begin living our life together as a new and happy family. As you might have guessed, once we got married things began to change. My husband began to grow distant from me, spending less time with me and being less loving as time passed. Eventually, he became critical of me, telling me I was no longer good enough, pretty enough or smart enough. Then came the rage. Suddenly I realized a shocking and horrible truth. I had married my father. In my attempt to escape the clutches of one toxic relationship, I had run head-on into another.

It was then that a friend of mine told me about something called narcissistic personality disorder. As I began to study this condition, I realized that I was literally reading about my husband and my father. I also began to realize that, as a child, rather than being the cause of a toxic environment, I had actually been the victim of one. The more I studied toxic personalities and relationships, the more I began to understand my own personality and behavior. After all, my romantic relationship wasn't the only time I became submissive and servile. Almost all of my friendships in college were the same way. I strived to please everyone in any way I could. I really believed that the path to my happiness was in making everyone else happy. Now I realized why that mindset had found its way into my brain.

When I turned thirty-five, I decided that it was time to turn my attention to relationships and personality disorders. I went back to school and became a life coach. Since then, I have devoted my life to helping others who have gone through the same toxic and traumatic events that I did break free of the effects of those events. By sharing my experiences as well as my knowledge on the subject, I am able to help them overcome the low self-esteem, emotional barriers, and limiting beliefs that keep them from fulfilling their true potential. Every time I help someone else to heal their emotional wounds, I feel as though I recover a little more myself. Perhaps that is the greatest gift I have found in helping others.

I am now living a happy, fulfilling life as a mother of two wonderful daughters. My daughters are strong, independent, and loving young women, a sign that I was able to overcome my past and be the parent I never had. As satisfying as that is, it isn't enough for me. I have recently come to the realization that I need to take my game up a level, so to speak. Instead of helping one or two people at a time, I need to help as many people as I can. This book is how I intend on doing just that. By sharing my experiences, insights, and knowledge in this book, I hope to help countless people to break free from their traumatic past and begin to live the happy, healthy life they are capable of. Furthermore, I hope to enable every reader to become the parents they dreamed of having when they were a child growing up with emotionally immature parents. If I can help others to experience the happiness, freedom, and sense of self-worth I have achieved, then I will have succeeded in my mission.

CHAPTER 2

What is Emotional Immaturity?

When you hear the term "emotional immaturity" you probably think of a small child, five or six years old, throwing a tantrum. Maybe their parents told them they couldn't buy a particular toy, or that they couldn't have hot dogs for lunch. No matter the reason, rather than simply accepting the situation and moving on, the child stomps their foot in protest, venting their frustration through shouting, crying, or the screaming that every parent dreads. While this is a very accurate portrayal of emotional immaturity, it is one that is hardly concerning. After all, children are immature. Therefore no one would expect them to understand why their behavior in such a situation was wrong.

Unfortunately, emotional immaturity does not always end when a person enters adulthood. Instead, it often follows an individual throughout their whole life, resulting in them acting in ways that are disrupting at best and harmful at worst, affecting every relationship they have in a very negative way. This chapter will discuss what it means to be emotionally immature, providing specific examples of behaviors and personality traits within emotionally immature people. It will also address some of the basic elements of emotional immaturity in parents, thereby helping you to know whether or not your parents meet those criteria.

Defining emotional immaturity

In order to fully understand what it means to be emotionally immature, you have to recognize that there are two distinct elements of this condition. The first element is the emotional one. When a person is emotionally immature, they often lack the ability to see life in an intellectual way. Instead, everything they experience is processed through an emotional filter, giving it a value strictly based on how it makes them feel. In other words, rather than thinking their way through life, an emotionally immature person *feels* their way through life. Therefore, in order for something to be good, it has to bring them pleasure. However, if a person, event, or experience fails to produce pleasure, it is seen as bad, wrong, or undesirable.

The second element of emotional immaturity is that of being immature. This covers a wide range of behaviors and personalities, all of which will be discussed in greater detail below. It is enough to understand at this point that the immature element of this condition keeps a person wholly self-absorbed, just like the average five or six-year-old child. Someone suffering from emotional immaturity is largely incapable of seeing beyond their own thoughts and feelings. As a result, they often ignore big-picture issues such as world events, common causes, and other things that serve to bring meaning to the world as a whole. Their entire existence takes place within their own mind, consisting only of their desires, fears, and expectations. Such a self-centered mindset results in the inability to see life from another person's perspective, resulting in every decision, action, and response being highly selfish in nature.

When combined, both elements create a third component, that of being unable to control emotional responses, both good and bad. This is where the image of the child throwing a temper tantrum comes into play again. Rather than considering other people's feelings or the consequences of their own actions, an emotionally immature person will simply act out their emotional response to any situation that triggers them. Usually, this is seen in episodes of rage where a person will literally explode when they don't get their own way. While the tantrums of a child are little more than annoying, those of a grown adult can be terrifying, especially when they are capable of causing serious harm or injury to others. Subsequently, it is vital to know the warning signs of an emotionally immature person in order to better protect yourself from any potential outbursts they may engage in.

Emotional immaturity in parents

Experiencing emotional immaturity in a person is bad enough under any circumstances. When it is experienced in one's own parents, it becomes immeasurably worse. This is because the relationship between a child and their parents is one of dependency, wherein the child relies on their parents to provide love, direction and most importantly, protection from all forms of harm and danger. When those parents are emotionally immature, it leaves the child not only vulnerable to the dangers of the outside world; it also leaves them vulnerable to the dangers their own parents create. This can cause significant emotional trauma, the scars of which can last a lifetime. Telltale signs that your parents are emotionally immature, include the following:

- **They are self-centered.** People, in general, can tend to be a bit self-centered, choosing to do things that serve their interests first before acting on behalf of others. However, when someone becomes a parent, that mindset is expected to change. While the individual can still put their needs and the needs of their family first, they should never put their personal desires over the needs of their own children. Yet this is a classic sign that a parent is emotionally immature.

- **They are inconsistent.** Another expectation of a good parent is that they be consistent in their mood, their values, and their actions. By being consistent, they help create an environment that feels safe and secure for their children. In contrast, when a parent experiences extreme mood swings, or they become erratic in their behavior, it creates a sense of chaos that undermines a child's sense of security and trust. Never knowing what to expect from a parent is enough to cause any child to retreat into the safety of their own mind, becoming closed off to others as a result.

- **They are easily stressed.** No one would argue that the life of a parent is easy and stress-free. On the contrary, every parent who cares about their children and their home will experience stresses of all shapes and sizes on a daily basis. However, most parents develop a thick skin and the fortitude that enables them to withstand such stresses and live a happy, normal life. Unfortunately, this isn't how things work in the case of emotionally immature parents. Rather than becoming more resilient to stress, emotionally immature parents are highly vulnerable to stressful situations. On the one hand, this can cause them to become emotionally triggered by the slightest issue. On the other hand, it can cause them to run away from serious issues in life, burying their head in the proverbial sand rather than providing the guidance and support expected of them.

- **They are passive-aggressive or even aggressive toward their children.** This is something you would expect from a person who is emotionally immature. Thinking back to the child throwing a temper tantrum, one of the things that usually takes place in such a tantrum is a verbal rant of how the child hates their parents and how unfair their parents always are. Such outbursts are commonplace between children and emotionally immature parents. Unfortunately, in this case, it is the parent ranting to the child rather than the other way around. Alternatively, a parent might be more passive-aggressive, choosing to question the child's love for them when they feel they aren't getting their way. In either case, such emotional abuse can leave deep and painful scars.

- **They live vicariously through their children.** A common passive-aggressive tendency of emotionally immature parents is to live vicariously through their children. While any parent wants to share the joys and successes of their children, it is another thing altogether to try to experience those joys and successes firsthand. Emotionally immature parents will usually impose their choices and desires on their children, forcing them to live the life they were never able to live. This often happens when parents came from low-income families where opportunities were few and far between. It frequently shows up in such things as career choices or which college to attend, where the parent puts their dreams over those of their child.

- **They create an overly dependent relationship.** Any child will be dependent on their parents to a large extent. After all, few children can put a roof over their heads and food on the table, so they will necessarily rely on the efforts of their parents. However, emotionally immature parents will use this dependency to their advantage, creating a situation where they become more and more necessary in their child's life. Instead of building a mindset of confidence and independence in their child, emotionally immature parents keep the child in a state of need, ever-relying on them for security and support. This inflates the importance of the parent, bringing value and meaning to their life at the expense of their child.

Ten signs of emotional immaturity

The previous list focused on the signs exhibited by emotionally immature parents toward their own children. It is important to remember that while a person might be a parent, they are still very much a regular person as well. This means that their emotional immaturity will affect every aspect of their life, not just their relationships at home. Subsequently, there are numerous other signs of emotional immaturity that can be witnessed in all areas of life, including work, social relationships, and the like. The following list is ten of the most common signs that a person is emotionally immature.

1. They never take responsibility for their actions

One of the biggest signs of maturity in a person is their ability to own up to their actions, especially when those actions bring negative consequences. When a person lacks emotional maturity, however, that ability is usually completely missing. More often than not, this takes the shape of blaming other people or forces for the issue at hand. For example, if they lose their job because their job performance was poor, rather than taking responsibility, they will blame their boss or blame the economy for losing their job. They will never admit fault even when the blame falls directly on their shoulders.

Another way an emotionally immature person deflects responsibility for their actions is to blame the impact other people have on them. In the example of someone losing their job, even if the individual admits that their performance was sub-standard, rather than taking responsibility, they will blame others for stressing them out or not being supportive enough, thereby causing them to be poor at their job. Thus, the fault can always be traced to someone else, even in an abstract and passive-aggressive way.

2. They lack empathy

It stands to reason that someone who is wholly consumed by their own emotional state of mind will be completely incapable of showing empathy toward anyone for any reason. Thus, an emotionally immature person is easy to spot as they are the most critical, uncaring, and seemingly heartless of people you will ever meet. In many cases, such a person is chalked off as cold-hearted, not caring about the pain and suffering of others. However, it's less a matter of not caring about the suffering of others and more a case of not actually seeing the suffering in the first place.

Since emotionally immature people live in their own world, they rarely take the time to look around them long enough to actually see the condition of others. Thus, rather than being uncaring, they are simply oblivious to what other people are going through. In short, if it doesn't affect them, it doesn't exist in their reality. Alternatively, when an emotionally immature person does witness the pain and suffering of others, they ignore it simply by habit. Since they are conditioned to put their needs and wants first, they have no time or energy to contemplate the needs and struggles of others. Again, it's less about being cold-hearted and more about simply being oblivious of other people.

3. They put other people down in order to gain power

Another common trait of emotionally immature people is that of putting other people down in order to gain power. More often than not, this is an issue of low self-esteem, wherein the individual feels incapable of proving themselves worthwhile and thus relies on pointing out other people's faults in order to look better. A common environment where this occurs is in the workplace. An employee who feels insecure will be more apt to talk about the faults of others in order to improve their own image. This might be nothing more than an attempt to gain positive recognition; however, such behavior can also be used to gain promotion at someone else's expense.

Needless to say, putting down others to gain prestige or power is a practice used by emotionally immature people in the more intimate environment of the home as well. Whether it's belittling a spouse or a child, such behavior serves the same function of making an insecure person feel better about themselves. More often than not, the things they criticize in others are traits they possess in abundance. Thus, they may be apt to complain that no one ever considers their needs when making decisions, or that no one cares about how they feel. In the end, they will usually project their own shortcomings onto others, something that creates an overwhelming sense of irony as well as despair.

4. They reject the opinions of others (get defensive)

Emotionally immature people are usually among the most defensive people you will ever meet. It is almost impossible to have a meaningful conversation with them as they are apt to reject other people's opinions when those opinions differ from their own. This is another example of a behavior that can be found in both people suffering from low self-confidence and those considered emotionally insecure. Rather than being able to entertain another person's opinion, an emotionally immature person must always be seen to be right. Therefore, they will always argue until they feel they have won the debate, even if there was no debate in the first place.

5. They always put their needs first (stuck in toddler state)

As mentioned earlier, another common trait of an emotionally immature person is to always put their needs first. This is another sign that the individual is emotionally stuck in the toddler state. Just as a toddler cannot see beyond their wants and needs, so too, an emotionally immature person has the same tunnel vision. Nothing else matters to them other than constantly finding pleasure and appeasement. This can be evidenced in such things as a child having worn-out shoes while their parents have brand new shoes, or a child having little more than a mattress to sleep on while the parents have a brand new TV in their bedroom. Overall, while most parents will sacrifice their own comfort and happiness in order to provide for their children, emotionally immature ones will sacrifice the happiness and wellbeing of their children in order to satisfy their own desires first.

6. They are incapable of compromise

At first glance, this trait may seem redundant to the trait of rejecting other people's opinions. After all, in order to be incapable of compromise, you have to be unwilling to consider the opinions of others. However, that's only half the equation here. The other half is that of an emotionally immature person, always putting their needs first. Therefore, the inability to compromise can be seen as a composite of the need to be first and the need to be right. This results in the emotionally immature individual being unwilling to budge an inch, instead choosing the mindset of all or nothing. Even if the opinion or desire of the other party or parties is close to that of the emotionally immature person, it doesn't matter. Any compromise is seen as a sacrifice, and the idea of sacrifice is beyond comprehension to anyone who lacks emotional maturity.

7. They are uncaring of other people's feelings (me over we)

This corresponds with the lack of empathy already discussed in this section. However, a lack of empathy can usually be attributed to a state of being oblivious to others, whereas being uncaring of other people's feelings is something different. In this case, the emotionally immature person is wholly aware of the emotional distress of others; however they choose to put themselves first nonetheless. While this may indicate heartlessness and even a sadistic tendency in some instances, for the most part, it reveals just how detached from reality the individual is. More often than not, the reason an emotionally immature person is uncaring of other people's feelings is that they are certain that when they are happy, everyone will be happy. Therefore, the best course is to pursue their own happiness, no matter how that affects others. An emotionally immature person truly believes that if they are happy and others are unhappy, it is the fault of others for being unreasonable or stubborn, not the other way around.

8. They have difficulty talking about their personal feelings

Ironically enough, one of the most common signs of emotional immaturity in a person is their inability to talk about their personal feelings. You would expect the opposite to be true, especially in light of how important an emotionally immature person's feelings are to them.

However, rather than wanting to talk about their feelings, they choose to avoid such conversations, either changing the subject or becoming sarcastic in an attempt to downplay the significance of the topic. This results in an inability to establish any real connection with the individual, making it impossible to change their emotionally immature outlook on life. Therefore, this can be seen as a defense mechanism of sorts, protecting the "child" from the outside world.

Another explanation, however, is a bit more sinister in nature. This suggests that the emotionally immature person is somehow aware of the fact that they aren't behaving right. Subsequently, they choose to avoid conversations that might force them to evaluate their mindset and recognize their shortcomings. As these people always need to be right anything that might reveal character flaws is seen as taboo, and thus avoided at all costs.

9. They avoid talking about the future

Something that sets children apart from adults is their ability to be wholly present in the moment. For the most part, this is a positive thing, allowing a child to experience life in depth that adults are usually unable to share. However, the average person outgrows this ability as they begin to become more responsible in life. Such things as getting a job, looking for a home, and even looking for a partner in life cause the average person to spend a lot of time and energy thinking about the future. Since emotionally immature people shirk responsibility, they lack the need to think about the future. Subsequently, they will usually avoid any conversation that requires making plans, considering outcomes, or any other element relating to the future.

10. They hold on to the past

Unfortunately, although emotionally immature people are unwilling to face the future, they are equally unwilling to let go of the past. This is especially true with regards to holding grudges. If an emotionally immature person feels as though they have been wronged, they will hold on to that feeling permanently. No matter what the other person does to make amends, they will never be fully forgiven. One reason for this is that emotionally immature people are unable to let go of their own traumatic experiences, no matter how trivial or self-created they may be. Therefore, if you ever hurt their feelings in even the slightest way, you will be marked for life.

Another reason why an emotionally immature person will hold on to the past is for leverage. They will bring up any past mistake or wrongdoing to gain emotional power over another person, using guilt and regret to manipulate them. This is the foundation on which emotional abuse is built. However, the same does not apply to the individual themselves. Instead of holding on to their own past mistakes and shortcomings, they will rewrite history, creating a narrative where they were right, and everyone else was wrong. This is another example of how detached from reality an emotionally immature person truly is.

CHAPTER 3

Different Types of Emotionally Immature Parents

Discovering that you are the product of emotionally immature parents can be a hard thing to accept, especially when you consider the implications such a discovery can have on your life. The chances are you are the victim of a stolen childhood, having been forced to grow up far sooner than most people need to and thus robbing you of the fun and innocence that is supposed to define your childhood years. Even worse, many of the wounds caused by your emotionally immature parents continue to cause pain and suffering even into adulthood, making it seem as though the harm your parents caused you is somehow inescapable. Fortunately, the discovery that your parents are emotionally immature is the first step in the healing process. This step helps you to realize that your emotional struggles are not actually your fault.

The next step in the healing process is to determine exactly what kind of emotional immaturity your parents expressed. Just as an individual can experience numerous types of emotions, so too, they can also exhibit numerous types of emotional immaturity. These different types can be broken down into four main groups, each of which has a unique form of behavior associated with it. Some parents may be more manipulative, whereas others may be more absent from their child's life altogether. Alternatively, some parents can be outright critical of their children, creating a sense of never being good enough that follows them all through life. By better understanding the type of emotionally immature parents, you have, you can better understand the impact they have on your emotional, mental, and even physical wellbeing. This chapter will present the four main types of emotionally immature parents, along with the nature of the relationship they have with their children. Furthermore, it will describe some of the most common effects those relationships have on the child's life, even as an adult. The four most common types of emotionally immature parents are as follows:

1. Emotional parents

Emotional parents are those who demonstrate their emotional state without any type of control whatsoever. This means that they can exhibit everything from extreme rage to extreme sorrow, and from extreme depression to extreme joy. At first glance the idea of expressing extreme joy may not seem like such a bad thing, however, in this context it only adds to the confusion and uncertainty of the emotional environment, causing the child to feel highly insecure as a result. However, it's the other emotions that are of particular concern as they are dangerous in even the best of circumstances.

When an emotional parent feels rage, they can release their rage without warning, going into violent fits of shouting, breaking objects, and even hitting people. Needless to say, none of these scenarios is healthy for anyone, most especially a young child who is both vulnerable and incapable of truly understanding what they are witnessing. In the case of physical abuse, an emotional parent may strike out at a child anytime that child does something considered wrong. What makes this abuse even worse is that the parent will explain why the child is responsible for making them angry in the first place. Thus, not only does the child suffer from the pain of being physically abused, but they also suffer from the pain of guilt, feeling as though the whole experience is their fault. Anyone who goes through this type of upbringing will have deep emotional scars. Many will struggle with their emotions. As a result, seeing any feeling of anger as something dangerous and shameful. Even worse, many resist having families of their own as they are afraid that they may turn out like their emotional parents and cause harm to their own children.

Most of the time, emotional parents aren't physically abusive. This doesn't mean that their actions are any less damaging to their children. On the contrary, the wounds of emotional abuse can cause pain long after the pain of physical trauma has become nothing but a distant memory. In the case of parents showing extreme sadness or depression, it can affect a child very deeply as they often are made to feel responsible for those emotional states. A common form of this is when a parent becomes irrationally sad over their child's behavior, and tells that child that they are to blame. Needless to say, children are going to do and say things that they never would as an adult. Any good parent will allow such instances to slide, seeing as it's all a part of the growing process. Unfortunately, emotional parents will take such events personally, responding the way they would if it were an adult instead of their child who was acting out. This causes the child to feel deep regret and guilt, things no child should ever experience. If these situations occur on a regular basis, it can significantly undermine a child's sense of self-worth, causing serious issues throughout their adult life.

Perhaps the greatest effect emotional parents have on their children is the sense of anxiety that comes from a highly charged emotional environment. Any time a child is afraid of setting their parents off, they can feel as though they are constantly walking on eggshells. Rather than being able to enjoy life and explore their own being, children of emotional parents are on a perpetual state of alert, watching their every word and action in case they might cause their parents to go off on a tangent. This never-ending state of self-scrutiny can lead to a person being self-conscious all throughout their life. They can become indecisive, fearing all possible negative consequences to any action they take. Furthermore, they may feel personally responsible for the happiness of those around them, as though they alone determine how everyone else feels and thinks at any given time.

2. Driven parents

Driven parents are a lot less unpredictable and unstable than emotional parents. However, the impact they have on their children can be no less severe and painful. For the most part, parents in this category are highly ambitious with professional careers in fields such as medicine, the law, and even politics. While there is no question that instilling ambition and a sense of purpose in a child is a good and healthy thing, these parents take it to a level that is devastating to a young mind. In short, driven parents are the perfectionists who never allow their children to be anything other than young adults who are expected to be better than the rest.

A child who grows up with driven parents is one who will be robbed of their childhood for certain. Instead of being able to play like other children—running around, making noise, rolling in the dirt and just generally be carefree and young, they will have to act as though they were an adult in a child's body. Their parents will usually forbid them to make a lot of noise, indoors or even outside, and they will definitely not be allowed to get dirty like the average child. Worse still, they will be expected to care for their toys as though they were museum curators caring for ancient and precious artifacts. While other kids can beat their toys around, crashing cars and losing pieces to action figures, these children will be reprimanded if their toys lose their "just out of the box" look and smell. In fact, some children will even be prohibited from taking their toys out of the box as that would only lead to them getting worn, damaged, or lost.

This sense of expectation goes far beyond just clothing, behavior, and toys. Driven parents will expect nothing but the highest grades from their children in every subject they study. Despite the fact that only a fraction of the population is naturally capable of scoring the best grades in every area, children of driven parents will be relentlessly held to this standard. Furthermore, their behavior in school will need to be exceptional. In many cases, it isn't even enough for the child to simply be well behaved and off the radar. Instead, they are expected to be so exceptional that teachers will remark about their perfect behavior, heaping praise more on the parents than on the child themselves.

Unfortunately, no matter how hard a child tries, more often than not, they will fall well short of the expectations set by their driven parents. The constant struggle for perfection, coupled with never being good enough in their parents' eyes, will usually result in the child being high-strung throughout their adult life, constantly feeling inadequate for not being the absolute best. Such people are always hard on themselves, being highly self-critical any time they fall short of absolute perfection. They will always feel as though they could have and should have done better, and they will never be satisfied with themselves the same way that their parents never were.

In some cases, this can translate into a person being highly critical of other people, finding fault in the smallest of details. Such criticism can do serious harm to friendships and even relationships of a more intimate nature. However, most children of driven parents usually just suffer from the feeling that they will never meet the expectations of others, causing them to form few, if any, close personal relationships. Furthermore, they will usually be uptight, never allowing themselves to let their hair down and have some real fun. This can keep them from enjoying their lives in a real and meaningful way, thereby robbing them of the happiness they truly deserve.

3. Passive parents

The third type of emotionally immature parent is that of the passive parent. These are the parents who are present in the body, but seemingly always absent in spirit. They rarely show emotions of any kind, positive or negative, regardless of the situation. While this can be seen as far less traumatic than the overbearing emotions of emotional parents, it can still cause a significant amount of damage nonetheless.

Most children of passive parents will tend to feel unwanted and alone. This is because their parents failed to give them the emotional support and love they needed at their most vulnerable and influential time. This isn't to say that the parents don't love their children for any sinister reason, rather it is usually the result of the parents being relatively incapable of feeling love in any real and meaningful way. Since they can't feel the same depth of emotion that emotionally healthy people feel they seem passive and detached in their behavior. Any adult would be able to chalk off such distance as a quirk. However, the average child can take it personally, making them feel unwanted and unloved.

For the most part, passive parents aren't bad parents, neglecting the day-to-day needs of their children or abusing their children physically, emotionally, or otherwise. Instead, they simply fail to provide their children with any real sense of emotional warmth and comfort. While they don't instill fear or insecurity, they also don't instill love or joy. Passive parents never form a close emotional attachment to their children that makes their children feel as though they belong in their home and family. Instead, passive parents co-exist with their children, seeing them as just other people in their lives, like tiny roommates that they only acknowledge with a cordial "hello" and maybe a smile.

Not only can this lack of connection make a child feel unloved, but it can also serve to stunt the emotional growth of the child, impacting their ability to have meaningful relationships as an adult. Only when a child experiences emotions can they begin to explore and develop those emotions. When they lack the interaction necessary for that process, their emotional growth can end before it even starts. Worse still, as most children look to their parents as examples to follow, children of passive parents may suppress their emotions, seeing them as foolish or unimportant. This can cause them to lack the ability to fall in love and start a family of their own later in life. Alternatively, if they do start a family, it will probably resemble that of their childhood, one lacking emotional connection and depth, thereby making their spouse and children feel unloved and alone.

4. Rejecting parents

Finally, there are the rejecting parents. These can be the most negative parents in a way, rivaling the emotional parents in the abuse and harm they cause. While emotional parents can exhibit positive as well as negative behavior, rejecting parents are almost solely negative in nature. This creates serious issues for any child being brought up by such people, resulting in emotional trauma that can lead to rebellious behavior up to and including criminal activity. Needless to say, any child of rejecting parents has a long road to recovery ahead of them.

One of the most common traits of rejecting parents is the tendency to degrade their children. This often comes in the form of calling their children such things as "stupid", "ugly", "fat" or any other word that humiliates and shames their child. While many parents may use such language from time to time in a joking manner, rejecting parents will use such terms on a regular basis, thus programming the child to believe that they are in fact stupid, ugly and generally undesirable. In many cases, such children grow up with virtually no self-esteem, feeling as though they have nothing to offer the world. In extreme cases, this lack of self-esteem can take the form of self-loathing, leading a person to literally hate everything about themselves. Such people can fall into self-destructive behaviors, such as harming themselves physically or destroying relationships that would otherwise be happy and fulfilling.

Another way that rejecting parents can exhibit their negativity is in putting the needs of their child last. Such parents will always say such things as "Not now", or "Stop bothering me" when their child comes to them for help, comfort or just companionship. While this may not seem as harmful as calling a child stupid or ugly, it is in fact just as damaging to a child's psyche. The end result is that the child feels unwanted and unloved, much the way they might with passive parents. What makes this scenario worse is that the child of rejecting parents recognizes that their parents consider other things more important than the child. For example, the parent might tell their child to stop bothering them while they are watching TV. This will make the child recognize that they are less important to their parents than the fictional characters on a TV show. This feeling can lead to all sorts of problems down the road.

One way that children of rejecting parents respond to feeling unwanted is to rebel. From an early age, they may act out by misbehaving in any way they can imagine. Acts of vandalism, violence, and antisocial behavior are commonplace among children of rejecting parents. While the defiance alone is part of the reason for this behavior, another reason is to get the attention they crave. Since normal behavior fails to get them noticed they resort to abnormal behavior. This doesn't mean that the child is necessarily given to violence or criminal activity, rather it means they are so starved of attention and affection that they will do almost anything to get it, even if it results in negative attention. In their mind, any attention is better than no attention at all.

Another outcome is that children of rejecting parents will gravitate to any attention they are given, regardless of who it comes from. This makes them highly vulnerable to predators who would take advantage of them, both at a young age and in adult life. Many children of rejecting parents will wind up with abusive spouses. Although they may suffer as a result of the abuse, they will never leave the relationship, fearing that they will forever be alone if they did. Thus, they will endure the most horrendous abuses if it means they get attention, even if it is attention of the wrong kind. Furthermore, their lack of self-esteem makes them feel as though such a relationship is the only kind they are worthy of, so they accept it as if it is the best they could hope for.

CHAPTER 4

The Consequences of Growing Up with Emotionally Immature Parents

The importance of a person's childhood years cannot be overstated. It is during those early years that a person develops their personality, behaviors, beliefs, and interpersonal relationship skills. When a person is raised in a loving and caring environment, they are given the best chance for developing in a healthy and positive way. They are able to create and maintain strong, loving relationships, they are self-assured and secure in their abilities, and they have a healthy appreciation for life, and all that life has to offer.

Unfortunately, when a person grows up with emotionally immature parents, their development is far less positive and successful. Such people struggle to develop healthy and loving relationships that stand the test of time, often becoming solitary or the prisoners of dysfunctional, abusive relationships. Additionally, they lack the self-confidence that a healthy childhood creates. In the end, the consequences of growing up with emotionally immature parents can be life-long, affecting a person well after they have left the confines of their childhood home.

This chapter will explore eight of the most common personality types that result from being raised by emotionally immature parents. It will define the personality type, pointing to possible events and environments that can cause a person to take on that particular type. It will also explain how these personality types act as a sort of defense mechanism with which to handle the pain of a traumatic upbringing. Finally, it will reveal the potential dangers inherent within each type, especially with regard to forming healthy and lasting relationships. The eight common personality types associated with children raised by emotionally immature parents are as follows:

1. **The loner**

Perhaps the most common of all personality types associated with people being raised by emotionally immature parents is that of the loner. Loners are those who detach themselves from society, choosing a life of solitude with few if any significant relationships. Such individuals are often prone to depression as they lack the social interaction that can help a person to stay motivated, positive, and full of energy. As a result, the joy and love they were robbed of as a child remains absent in their adult life as well.

Most loners come from parents who were passive in nature. As already discussed, such parents show little to no emotion toward their children. Thus their children struggle with feeling and showing emotion later in life. Additionally, those raised by passive parents probably feel detached from people in general, which is why they choose a life of isolation. It's not a matter of them rejecting society, or even being afraid of having relationships. Rather, it's that they became accustomed to being alone. Therefore they don't feel the need to have other people in their life.

The main outcome faced by loners is loneliness. No matter how independent a person is, the fact is that they need other people in their lives in order to thrive. Thus, loneliness and even depression are commonplace among those who pursue a life of solitude. Another consequence of being isolated is social anxiety. This usually occurs when a loner is forced to interact with other people, such as at school, work, or in a social environment where numerous people are interacting. While they may develop enough courage to face this anxiety when necessary, they will usually avoid any situation requiring them to interact with other people whenever possible. Social anxiety can even occur in the most mundane scenarios, such as grocery shopping, eating at a restaurant, or any other situation that finds a loner in a more crowded environment.

2. **The perfectionist**

More often than not, perfectionists are those who were raised by driven parents. Rather than being appreciated for who they were as children, perfectionists suffered the trauma of always being criticized by their parents, forever falling short of impossibly high expectations. Once out of the house, such people tend to carry the voices of their parents in their minds for the rest of their lives. Any time they try to accomplish something, they will hear one or both of their parents telling them how they could have done better, or been quicker or pursued a more worthwhile goal. Even though their parents may be long gone, their voices will continue to haunt their minds for the rest of their life.

A common side effect of perfectionists is the development of self-loathing. After all, it's hard to appreciate yourself when you are constantly defined as being substandard or even a failure. Eventually, that harsh criticism becomes internalized, creating not just low self-esteem, but outright self-loathing. On a lesser scale, most perfectionists are simply too hard on themselves, never being happy with their performance or their lives in general. This can result in them spending their lives trying to achieve a goal that no one can ever reach— perfection.

In addition to being too hard on themselves, perfectionists can also be overly critical of others. This can be a real issue when it comes to establishing significant interpersonal relationships, as their constant criticism can seem negative and spiteful to others. Ironically, not all perfectionists see their criticism as negative. Instead, they identify it as a paternal sign of affection. Thus, when others become frustrated with the constant nit-picking, the perfectionist can feel misunderstood. After all, in their mind, they were only trying to bring out the best in the other person, the way any loving parent or spouse would want to.

3. The social butterfly

Social butterflies are a personality type that can be hard to detect at first. Most of the time, these people seem super happy and outgoing; therefore, it's hard to see them as the byproduct of a dysfunctional upbringing. The telltale sign that a person is a social butterfly comes in the form of them being incapable of forming close, intimate relationships that are long-lasting. Therefore, the only people that discover that a person is a social butterfly are those who try to get close to them in a real and significant way.

People who fit the social butterfly category are usually those who had an emotionally stunted childhood. This can be the result of being raised by passive parents who failed to provide any deep and meaningful connection on an emotional level. However, a stunted emotional condition can also be the result of a child being raised by rejecting parents. A general lack of deep love and acceptance can result in a person never being able to get too emotionally involved with another person. For some, this is due to a fear of being rejected, later on; therefore, they leave a relationship when everything is still happy and good. Alternatively, it can simply be a person's inability to experience deep and lasting emotional attachments as they never developed them as a child.

While social butterflies can live productive and seemingly normal lives, they will always suffer the pain of never having a lasting and meaningful relationship that brings fulfillment and purpose in their lives. This isn't to say that they won't go through the motions, however. Many social butterflies defy expectation and actually get married, however such marriages rarely last, ending in divorce when it's time for the social butterfly to fly off to their next encounter.

4. The empath

Empaths are a rare breed, often coming from childhoods that are full of pain, abuse, and other significant traumas. More often than not, empaths are the offspring of emotional parents, those who created an emotionally unstable, unpredictable, and undesirable environment. Whether these parents were physically abusive or just emotionally abusive, the simple fact is that their children spent their most vulnerable years suffering from fear, confusion, and pain. It is this pain that usually drives a person to become an empath in the first place.

What sets empaths apart from ordinary people is their inherent ability to connect to the pain and suffering of another person. While many may see this as some sort of superpower, the dark truth is that it can be the consequence of a person having suffered severe pain and suffering in their own life. Only when a person knows pain can they relate to the pain of others. This ability to feel the pain of other people can cause an empath to ignore their own needs in order to fulfill another person's needs, thereby helping them to overcome or even avoid pain and suffering in the first place. Therefore, empaths are usually selfless, often to the point of putting themselves in danger either through self-neglect or by taking on more than they can handle in an attempt to help as many people as they can.

Empaths are usually very noble in nature, fighting for humanitarian causes and the like whenever they can. This nobility is at the very heart of their empathic personality itself. More often than not, a person becomes an empath in an attempt to rid the world of the pain and suffering they experienced as a child. They spend their lives trying to be the opposite of the parents that caused them such trauma, thus becoming the cure of pain and suffering rather than the cause. Unfortunately, this effort to be the opposite of their parents can consume them, resulting in a life spent running from their past and never creating a future for themselves. Although their efforts are positive in nature and usually positive in the outcome, most empaths suffer loneliness, depression and other emotional and psychological struggles due to their constant exposure to the pain and suffering of those around them.

5. The guilty one

A similar personality type to the empath is that of the guilty one. Unfortunately, this type puts a highly negative twist on the attempt to soothe the pain and suffering of others. Rather than simply trying to overcome and prevent pain, guilty ones actually take responsibility for the suffering of others. They feel as though pain and suffering is their fault; thus, they spend their whole life trying to please others as a sort of penance to atone for their guilt.

Children who grow up to be guilty ones may have been raised by rejecting parents, driven parents, or emotional parents. Those raised by rejecting parents can trace their guilt to the low self-esteem created by the constant rejection, degradation, and humiliation practiced by their parents. Such low self-esteem can cause a person to feel as though they adversely affect the lives of others simply by being present. A common consequence is that they feel responsible for the pain and suffering of others even when they are clearly not connected to that pain and suffering in any way, shape, or form.

Those raised by driven parents can trace their guilt to the trauma of never being considered good enough. The constant experience of falling short of expectations can cause a person to feel as though they are a disappointment to everyone, and that the pain and suffering of others are somehow due to their inadequacies. They will spend their lives trying to perfect the lives of others in any way they can, thereby eliminating pain and suffering.

More often than not, guilty ones are the byproduct of emotional parents. After all, it is a common trait of emotional parents to blame their anger, depression or sorrow on their children, thereby causing that child to feel responsible for the pain and suffering of everyone in their life. A child of emotional parents will thus blame themselves anytime someone else gets angry, upset, or depressed, even when there is no logical reason to do so. They simply feel that even if they didn't cause the pain, they didn't do enough to prevent it.

Guilty ones are destined to live a life defined by guilt and fear, constantly spending their time and energy trying to make amends for things that aren't their fault. The other people in their life may not even be abusive in nature, yet that won't stop the guilty one from reacting in the same manner that they did as a child when their parents blamed them for everything that went wrong. Unfortunately, this mindset will often cause a person to seek out an abusive relationship that allows them to act the only way they know how, in a constantly guilty and submissive role. Even worse, they will blame themselves when things go wrong in their own life, rather than allowing themselves to recognize the role other people and events play in how a person's life turns out.

6. The vampire

The term "vampire" can be used to describe a couple of different personality types. On the one hand, it can indicate a person who sucks the life out of others, constantly draining other people of their emotional, mental, and physical energy. They can be needy and dependent, or they can simply be so high-paced that other people struggle to keep up. In any event, they never invest energy in their relationships. Instead, they constantly take energy, much like a vampire draining the blood from their victim.

In this case, however, the term "vampire" is used to suggest that a person appears almost lifeless in terms of their emotions. Neither being alive nor truly dead, such people are the equivalent of the undead, emotionally speaking. Needless to say, vampires can usually trace their unemotional qualities back to their upbringing, which more often than not came at the hands of passive parents. The lack of emotional development during a person's childhood years often results in a fairly unemotional adult life.

Neither happy nor sad, the vampire simply exists in an emotionally lifeless state.

Vampires can lead fairly normal lives, holding down respectable jobs and being a benefit to society in general. The real issue comes from their ability to form strong emotional bonds with other people. Many vampires either choose to live a life of solitude, although not out of fear or revulsion of other people, as is the case with loners. Alternatively, vampires may form relationships with other vampires, resulting in an emotionally lackluster marriage that resembles the relationship of roommates rather than lovers.

7. The irrational thinker

Irrational thinkers are almost always the result of a child being raised by emotional parents. Unlike the guilty ones or the empaths, instead of devoting their lives to avoiding the emotional tumult of their parents, they perpetuate the cycle, bringing emotional devastation to the other people in their life. Irrational thinkers are those who mimic their emotional parents, often blaming those very parents for their emotional instability.

Needless to say, irrational thinkers are not hard to spot at all. They are the ones who perceive even the smallest of setbacks as monumental disasters. Known as catastrophizing, irrational thinkers will amplify any small problem into a virtual catastrophe. If the cups and plates don't match at the party, then the party is ruined. Or if the turkey is just a little on the dry side, Thanksgiving is ruined. In short, irrational thinkers will find any excuse to turn an otherwise ordinary or slightly less than ideal situation into a full-blown disaster, one in which they become enraged, blaming anyone and everyone for their self-created suffering.

Another common trait among irrational thinkers is to minimize the good in others, choosing instead to focus on their faults and shortcomings. Unlike the perfectionist who focuses on a person's imperfections for the sake of improvement, irrational thinkers focus on them for the sake of degrading the other person. In their mind, it's all or nothing, perfection or abject failure. Since no person, thing, or experience can ever be perfect, the irrational thinker has an infinite number of reasons to fly into a rage, depression, or any other negative emotion they choose. This includes paranoia, where they come to believe that the other people in their life are actively out to get them, ruining their life one insignificant act at a time.

8. The repressor

Finally, there are the repressors. These are the people who choose to repress their emotions, both good and bad, as they don't know how to express them in a healthy and productive way. More often than not, repressors are children of emotional parents. This stands to reason as, unlike children of passive parents, they actually possess strong emotions. Unfortunately, their childhood experience taught them the dangers of such strong emotions, especially those of anger, hate, and fear. However, unlike irrational thinkers, repressors are bound and determined to not become like their abusive parents who caused untold harm and suffering to them.

One common quality of repressors is the tendency to bottle up negative emotions such as anger. Rather than getting into an argument, or releasing their frustration on a matter, repressors will become uncharacteristically quiet when faced with negative emotions. This is because they are afraid they won't be able to control themselves if they allow their emotions to be expressed. Subsequently, they become silent and aloof for as long as the negative energy lasts. Eventually, they will come out of their "funk", interacting with people in a normal and healthy way again, but only when their anger and rage has dissipated completely.

At first glance, this may not seem a bad way to cope with being raised by emotionally abusive parents. Unfortunately, the passive appearance of this personality type hides a vicious undertone, one that often causes the repressor great emotional and even physical pain. The simple truth is that when a person represses or suppresses negative emotions, those emotions turn inward, causing a person to become angry with themselves. This anger can result in such things as depression, acts of self-harm, or even suicidal thoughts in more extreme cases. Even when emotional repression doesn't produce such severe emotional and psychological consequences, it can cause physical problems, such as ulcers, high blood pressure, and even an elevated risk of stroke. In the end, by not releasing their negative emotions and the pressure those emotions create, repressors turn into a time bomb of pent-up energy and pain waiting to either explode or otherwise totally consume themselves from the inside-out.

CHAPTER 5

Common "If" Thoughts and How to Change Them Trough Self-love

Most people make the all too common mistake of believing that their happiness is totally dependent on their circumstances. As a result, they develop a state of mind that focuses on what is known as "if" thoughts. These are the thoughts that say "I would be happy *if* only I had a better job", or "I would be happy *if* only I had more friends." The belief that circumstances can bring happiness is ingrained in the minds of most people through such mediums as advertising, where products, professions and even which credit card you use are shown to directly create the happiness you crave.

Unfortunately, this is nothing short of a bald-faced lie, one that serves to take advantage of people's misfortunes and unhappiness in order to sell merchandise and thus turn a profit. The simple truth is that while your job and your friends can affect your happiness, they cannot and will not actually *create* it. Happiness is a state of mind; as such, it comes from within, not from without. Therefore it is vital that you develop your happiness regardless of your external circumstances. The best way to achieve this is through self-love. This chapter will discuss some of the most common "if" thoughts, revealing their impact on a person's life, as well as how to change those thoughts by creating a mindset centered around contentment, gratitude and most importantly, self-love.

If I had a better career

If you ask the average person on the street whether or not they are happy with their job, only about half would say that they are. This means a full fifty percent of people are dissatisfied with their job to a significant degree. Some feel that they are overworked; others complain about being underpaid. Many people feel that their job is uninspiring, lacking any real sense of challenge, development, or personal growth. Despite these complaints, most people live relatively happy and fulfilling lives regardless of the job they have. However, this doesn't hold true for those with the "if" thought mindset. Those are the people who believe that their happiness is dependent on their career. Thus they live by the notion that they would be happier if only they had a better career.

Ordinarily, most people who wish for a better job want to feel satisfied with their work-life, or perhaps they want to make more money. However, in the case of people who were raised by emotionally immature parents, the reasons are different. These are the people who always feel ashamed, as though they are never good enough. In their mind, a better job will make them a better person, thus gaining the respect and affection that their parents never gave them. Unfortunately, no job ever provides the satisfaction they crave. Instead, the voices of their parents constantly ring out in their minds telling them they aren't good enough, no matter what job they have.

The only way to break this cycle of negativity is to realize that your parents aren't in charge anymore. You are. It is up to you to decide whether or not your job is good enough. It is for you to decide whether or not to look for something better. The most important thing is to recognize that, despite what your parents said, you are more than good enough. You are a truly wonderful person! While a better job might provide more money or more opportunities for growth, it won't make you more worthy of being happy. You deserve to be happy just as you are. This is the first step toward replacing your parents' judgment with self-love. Decide that you deserve happiness now, not later and not under different circumstances. Choose to find happiness in what you already have and in who you already are.

Another way of putting things into perspective is to recognize that your job isn't responsible for making you happy, rather it is responsible for providing you with the opportunity to earn an income. It's what you do with that income, and in your free time that is responsible for making your life a happy and fulfilling one. When you spend more time doing the things that make you happy, you take the pressure off of your job to provide meaning and contentment. Don't define your life by your job, instead define it by your interests, hobbies, and any activities that you enjoy doing. Those are the things that truly matter, as those reflect who you are as a person. The more time you spend doing things that bring happiness, the happier you will become over time. Eventually, you will replace the feeling of being inferior and unworthy of happiness with actual happiness and even a sense of purpose. As you continue to do the things you love, you will begin to love your life more and more as a result. This will provide an increased sense of self-love, something you truly deserve!

If I looked better

Another common "if" thought that countless people struggle with in life is the idea that they might be happier if only they looked better. What a truly horrible thought to have! If you really think about that for a moment, you realize that people are literally saying they aren't pretty enough to be happy. The really dark truth to consider is that advertising, yet again, is largely responsible for this mindset. How many commercials promise that you will find the man or woman of your dreams if only you buy their product and transform your otherwise plain appearance? Those commercials even show how much happier you will be with yourself once you look into the mirror and see someone looking back who is more attractive than you are now. Needless to say, this is a classic case of big companies preying on the vulnerability and fear of the average person in order to make a big profit.

While advertising is a big reason for most people feeling insecure about their looks, anyone raised by rejecting parents or driven parents will have other, more deep-seated reasons for feeling this way. Rejecting parents are always quick to criticize and humiliate their children in any way possible, and looks are no exception to this rule. In fact, most rejecting parents call their children fat, ugly, too skinny, or some other demeaning term that indicates some physical flaw setting them apart from the rest of the beautiful world. Even when they do so "in a joking way" as they sometimes claim, such criticisms go straight to a child's heart, undermining their self-image in ways that can last a lifetime. Driven parents are no better, often focusing on the few physical flaws their child might have rather than the countless aspects of beauty and wonder that they possess. This can cause a person to feel as though they are never good looking enough, even though others may envy their physical appearance. Again, the important thing is to break the cycle of self-loathing and begin to exercise the self-love that will bring true and meaningful happiness to your life.

The first step toward replacing the self-loathing your parents created with self-love is to change the dialogue in your mind. Most children of rejecting or driven parents constantly hear such things as "You aren't as pretty as everyone else", or "If only you were better looking." The only way to break free of these devastating criticisms is to replace them with positive, loving dialogue. Ask yourself what you wish your parents would have said to you. Perhaps you wish they would have said something like "You are the prettiest girl in the world", or "You are going to grow up to be such a handsome man!" Needless to say, every parent should say those things since they should see their children as the most wonderful things in existence.

The trick is to become the parent you wish you had. Look at yourself in the mirror and imagine the young child you once were. Then tell that child what they so desperately wanted to hear. Each and every time you look at yourself in the mirror, tell yourself that you are the cutest girl in the world, or that you are a handsome fellow. Love yourself the way your parents never did. This is how you replace the self-loathing dialogue with words of self-love and self-appreciation. Once the dialogue is replaced, your negative self-image will be replaced with a positive one, one that enables you to enjoy your life the way you both desire and deserve! It may take time to accomplish this goal. After all, you spent your entire childhood listening to the negative talk, so it will take a while to get your mind to accept the positive words it never heard before.

Another thing to consider is how foolish it is to equate your physical appearance with your ability to be happy. Again, this is where the advertising industry is so detrimental to the average person's wellbeing. Living in a culture that is dominated by materialism, consumerism, and physical appearance can cause even the most attractive and successful person to question their sense of self-worth. Therefore, another good practice is to recognize the fact that advertising campaigns associating beauty with happiness are nothing but lies. Every time you see a commercial promising happiness if you buy this or that product close your mind to it. In fact, go an extra step further and shout "Liar, liar!" at the TV, billboard or whatever it is you are looking at. This will remove the influencing impact such ad campaigns have on your sense of self-worth, leaving you to realize that you deserve to be happy and loved just as you are!

If I had more friends

Popularity is another currency that determines the value of a person's life in our materialistic culture. This stands to reason as the most popular people are usually the ones with more money, better jobs, and better looks. Therefore, how many friends a person has is often the measure of how happy or how successful they are. When you have more friends than you can, count you are seen as really successful. Alternatively, when there are only a few people, you consider true friends, you are perceived as a failure. The idea that the number of friends a person has equals the amount of happiness they experience isn't a new concept at all, but it is one that continues to cause as much damage in today's society as it has in countless societies in the past.

As with the other "if" thoughts, the idea that you would be happier if you had more friends can also be traced back to being raised by emotionally immature parents. People craving more friends are often the product of passive parents, those who paid little attention to their children, thus stunting their ability to socialize and develop significant friendships. While many children of passive parents grow up to be loners by choice, others become loners because that's all they know. By living a childhood bereft of emotional connections, a person becomes a stranger to such things. Thus, they are constantly an outsider looking in at a way of life they find strange and unfamiliar. In some cases, however, they may actually crave the ability to live such a life. This is especially true if they perceive such things as the number of friends a person has with the level of happiness they can achieve. The trick here is to break out of the mindset your parents created and begin to develop a healthier, more self-loving mindset.

While having more friends may not actually be the difference between being happy or unhappy, the truth of the matter is that having friends is never a bad thing. Therefore, if you find that the act of making friends terrifies you, or that you feel undeserving of having friends, you need to begin to change your sense of self-worth. The first step is to tell yourself that you deserve to be happy, and if that means having friends, then you deserve to have friends. Only when you open yourself up to letting others in can you begin the process of making more friends.

The next step is to actually start making friends. More often than not, this starts by meeting a person and simply getting to know them. Making friendly conversation while standing in line at the grocery store, or chatting with the barista at the coffee shop are easy and safe ways to establish contact with other people. The more comfortable you become with this, the more confident you will become in who you are. This will enable you to open up to other people so that you can form deeper, more meaningful friendships with them. Start spending time in more social environments, such as small parties or get-togethers where you can meet even more people and start making new friends. In the end, it's all about stepping outside your comfort zone and discovering a fascinating and vibrant new world. The most important thing to do, however, is, to be honest about who you are. If you struggle with opening up to new people simply tell them as much. Any decent person will understand social anxiety, and will usually adapt their behavior to ensure you are comfortable and happy.

While making more friends may actually lead to more happiness, it isn't necessarily always so. This is especially true in the event that you already have a large number of friends. One of the common threads of the "if" thought state of mind is the idea that more, bigger and better lead to a greater sense of happiness. In other words, having more money, better looks, or a bigger house will somehow change your life miraculously and bring you the happiness and satisfaction you crave. Unfortunately, there is no end to this way of thinking. It is an endless pursuit that has no final destination. In a way, it's a bit like a race with no finish line. You just keep running, faster and faster, further and further, and you never stop. The only way to stop running the endless race is to eliminate the mindset that the answer is always just ahead. Truly happy people are those who appreciate what they have, where they are, and most importantly, *who* they are. Only when you achieve this mindset can you stop chasing the goal that is perpetually beyond reach.

If I lived somewhere else

Location, location, location. That is the mantra of any business. In order to be successful, it is imperative that you place your business in the perfect location. Everything else is secondary. You can have the best product in the world. You might even be selling that product at the lowest price in the world. All of that is of no consequence if your business isn't in the right place. Therefore, where you are is more important than anything else. Unfortunately, many people believe that this rule applies to happiness as well as to business success. This leads to the idea that a person would be happy if only they lived somewhere else. While the location may be everything when it comes to creating a successful business, it won't actually make the difference for anyone who is unhappy with their life. At best it will only provide a temporary high, followed by a return to general dissatisfaction with life. At worst, it will lead a person to feel as though happiness is unachievable, thus resulting in depression and even suicidal thoughts.

In order to replace this mindset with one that is more positive and constructive, it is first necessary to understand where this idea came from in the first place. More often than not, any notion that happiness can only be achieved by acquiring something better than what you already have comes from driven parents. As mentioned earlier in this book, driven parents are those who are never satisfied. In their mind, things could always be better in one way or another, and they will not rest until those improvements are made. Unfortunately, there never is a time or place that is ever good enough. Therefore, happiness is always beyond reach.

If this is the mindset that you struggle with, it is vital that you recognize that happiness is a state of being, and it must be established in the here and now. This isn't to say that you shouldn't ever dream about being somewhere else or doing something else, rather it means that changing things in life won't ever create happiness, rather it will only increase the happiness you already have. Therefore, it is critical that you find happiness where you are with the life you already have. Otherwise, you will only take your sense of restlessness and dissatisfaction with you wherever you go, making even the best place a disappointment when it fails to provide the results you expected it to.

The trick, in this case, is to focus on the good aspects of your life rather than the bad. Any child of driven parents will be programmed to fixate on the bad rather than the good. This is the opposite of self-love or any other kind of love for that matter. Someone who fills their heart and mind with love will find the beauty in all things, not the flaws. They will find a reason to be happy even when circumstances aren't at their best. Furthermore, they will find reasons to be happy wherever they live. Sure, you might have a dream where you live in a particular place such as the beach, the mountains or in some exciting and vibrant city. However, that isn't to say you can't find contentment where you currently live. The important thing is to look for reasons to be happy, not reasons to be disappointed. What makes driven parents so harmful is that they can take a score of ninety-five percent and focus more on the five points lost than the ninety-five points earned. This creates a mindset that feels unsatisfied, even when things are overwhelmingly positive. Only by removing that mindset will a person ever be able to experience happiness in any real measure. Therefore, learn to love where you are, focusing on all the positives rather than on all the negatives. When you develop that ability, it will enable you to appreciate all the positive aspects of yourself, thereby replacing the self-criticism with a healthy sense of self-worth. This will enable you to be happy no matter where you are.

WAIT !!!
READ THIS BEFORE GOING ANY FURTHER!

How would you like to get your next eBook **FREE** <u>and</u> get new books for **FREE** too before they are publicly released?

Join our Self Empowerment Team today and receive your next (and future) books for **FREE**! Signing up is easy and completely free!!

Check out this page for more info!

www.SelfEmpowermentTeam.com/SignUp

Just a Friendly Reminder...

I'd like to offer you this amazing resource which my clients pay for. It is a report I written when I first began my journey.

Click on the picture above or navigate to the website below to join my exclusive email list. Upon joining, you will receive this incredible report on how to recognize an abusive relationship.

If you ask most people on the street what an abusive relationship is, chances are you'd get a description of physical abuse. And yes, that is most certainly an abusive relationship. However, abuse comes in many forms. The actual meaning of abuse is when someone exerts control over another person.

Find out more about recognizing an abusive relationship and learn how to take control over your life by clicking on the book above or by going to this link:

http://bit.ly/RecognizeAbusiveRelationship

CHAPTER 6

Four Steps to Inner-Healing

So far, this book has discussed the different types of emotionally immature parents and the various ways that they can impact a person's life. While discovering the true nature of your childhood trauma is a critical step in the healing process, it is only the first step. The next step is to begin to take control of your emotional wellbeing, thereby ending the control that your emotionally immature parents have over you. There are several ways to achieve this goal, each with a unique approach to handling the emotional traumas you are struggling with. This chapter will reveal four specific steps that will lead to the inner-healing you both crave and deserve. Each individual step will produce measurable, life-changing results that will improve your overall wellbeing exponentially. However, by combining all four steps, you will achieve a level of inner-healing that affects every part of your life, including your feelings, thoughts, and even physical wellbeing. Therefore, it is recommended that you take the time and effort to accomplish each of the four steps covered in this chapter. The four steps that will lead you to inner-healing are as follows:

1. **Develop detachment**

There are numerous religious and philosophical traditions in the world that try to help a person overcome the pain and suffering they experience in life. One of the most common methods for achieving this goal is to develop detachment. At first, this may sound a bit mechanical in nature, as though you are trying to shut off your emotions and become a virtual android who feels neither pain nor joy. However, this isn't the purpose of detachment at all. Instead, detachment is a skill that a person can develop to protect them from harmful influences, specifically people who actively seek to cause emotional pain and suffering. Thus, by developing detachment, you can start your road to inner-healing by preventing any further emotional trauma from taking place. In a way, you can think of this as damage control. Once you prevent further damage from occurring, you can begin to repair the damage that has already been done.

The first step is to develop detachment from the emotional influences your parents have on you. This won't be a quick fix. Rather, it will take constant and continual effort on your part. You can think of it like developing physical strength. No one would expect to walk into a gym as an ordinary person and walk out, looking like a bodybuilder after only one or two sessions. The more strength you want to achieve is the more effort it will take. This applies to emotional strength as well. Therefore, it is vital that you commit yourself to the process, investing the time, energy, and willpower needed to see you achieve the success that will change your life forever.

An effective method for developing this detachment is to visualize the act of kicking your parents out of your mind. Simply imagine your mind as a house where you live. Your parents have invaded your space, making demands and changes in your home that you aren't happy with. Instead of accepting that and letting them run your personal space, you choose to throw them out, thereby regaining control of your home and the life you live within it. Take the time to clearly imagine the process of kicking your parents out and slamming the door behind them.

At first, this may seem like a mere fantasy or wish fulfillment, but it is, in fact, a great deal more. The image of throwing your parents out of your 'home' is the first step to rewiring your mind so that it sees your parents on the outside rather than on the inside. As long as you allow your parents access to your mental and emotional wellbeing, they will take control away from you. However, once you kick them out, you regain control over your thoughts and feelings. Not only does this put you in charge, but it also eliminates the impact that your parents' words and actions have on your state of mind.

Although you can't change the way your parents behave, you can eliminate the impact that behavior has on you. By kicking them out of your mind you can tune out their words and actions, thus feeling safe inside your mind from the harm they would otherwise cause, just as you feel safe from unwanted people who are firmly shut out of your home. The important thing is to keep the image of your parents being kicked out fresh in your mind. You can even create mantras to help you maintain this mindset, such as "You aren't welcome in my home anymore", or "You don't control me anymore." These mantras will remind you that your parents are on the outside, leaving you safe and secure on the inside.

2. Process your grief

One of the most devastating elements of emotional trauma is the grief that it creates. This grief usually exists without the individual even being aware of it, making it all the more dangerous. The simple truth is that every child deserves love, comfort, and protection from their parents. When you don't receive these things, a big part of your soul becomes grief-stricken. Unfortunately, as a child, you don't always have the time nor the insight needed to address and process this grief. Instead, you have to develop the survival techniques that enable you to withstand the trauma of living with emotionally immature parents. However, as an adult who is seeking inner-healing from the traumas of your past, it is vital that you take the time and effort needed to process your grief.

A good way to do this is through visualization. Imagine that you are facing your parents in a heated argument. You have decided to hold them accountable for the pain and suffering they caused you as both a child and an adult. Take the time to create the situation in your mind carefully, and to think of all the things you want to say to your parents. Since this exercise can lead to a great deal of emotional release, it is important that you ensure you have plenty of time and privacy before beginning the process. Additionally, you will want to unplug or turn off any devices that could distract you from your visualization exercise.

Once you have established your space and the vision of your encounter you can play out the full story, including the things you want to say along with the arguments your parents would doubtlessly present were the situation happening for real. However, in this case, you hold all the cards. Your parents can only argue back if you allow them to, meaning you are in full control. Furthermore, you can say as much as you want, using the tone of voice that you want and even the language you want. As you argue with your parents, you should let yourself get as mad, upset, sad, or ferocious as possible. After all, the purpose of this exercise is to release pent up grief. Therefore you need to unleash your emotions and let them run wild.

If you really want a good work out, you can take this to the next level and use the empty chair technique. This is when you sit across from an empty chair, or two in this situation, and actually rehearse the scene verbally and physically, as though you were rehearsing for a play or a movie role. Again, it is important to feel comfortable doing this, therefore make sure you are totally alone and that no one can hear you shouting at your imaginary parents. Only when you feel totally free to express yourself will you be able to fully let go. By using the empty chair technique, you can shout, shake your fist, jump up and down, and do whatever else you would if you were actually having a full-blown argument with your parents. The more physical you get is, the more energy you will release, and this can go a long way to freeing your heart and mind of the grief and frustration that has weighed you down your entire life.

For even better results, you can follow up your confrontation with a movie that is a guaranteed tear-jerker. The movie can be any movie at all. It doesn't have to be about children of abusive or emotionally immature parents. All that matters is that you do a good bit of crying after your venting. This will help to release even more emotional energy that may be lingering beneath the surface. In the end, you want to come away from this experience feeling emotionally exhausted and spent, much the way you would feel physically exhausted after a triathlon or some other extreme challenge that consumed every ounce of physical energy you possessed. This will leave your heart and mind clear so that you can start replacing the negative thoughts and feelings with the thoughts and feelings of love, happiness, and self-esteem that you truly deserve.

3. Establish emotional boundaries

The third step to achieving inner-healing is to establish emotional boundaries. In order to appreciate how this works, it is necessary to explore the purpose of boundaries in general. The basic function that an established boundary serves is to create a sense of space. Anything within the boundary is good, desirable, or belongs to you. Anything on the outside of the boundary is bad, undesirable or someone else's. Furthermore, boundaries can also provide protection, such as fences, walls, and the like. Therefore, in addition to dividing good from bad or yours from theirs, boundaries can keep those things that are good and that belong to you safe from outside forces that would threaten them. This function holds true for boundaries of all kinds, including emotional boundaries.

When establishing emotional boundaries, the first thing to separate is your emotions from those of other people. This is especially true in the case of your parents. Since emotionally immature parents tend to generate negative emotions and the negative energy associated with them, it is vital to differentiate between their emotions and yours. When you discover thoughts and feelings that are bad or that don't belong to you it is essential that you put them out of your mind, creating the barrier that keeps them from invading your mind and undermining your emotional and mental health and wellbeing. Once you create this barrier, you will feel a weight lifted, as though an unwanted presence was suddenly gone from your life, taking with it the negativity you have been struggling with for so long.

Establishing this barrier is a simple process, but one that requires a little extra attention with regard to any emotions you experience. Simply put, each and every time you encounter an emotion or a particular state of mind, you need to take a moment to consider its origin. Is that emotion truly yours? Do those thoughts belong to you? Or, as is more often the case, can those thoughts and feelings be traced back to another source such as your emotionally immature parents? Every time you discover thoughts and feelings that don't belong to you, the trick is to let them go. You can go a step further and throw them out of your mind, slamming the door behind them to ensure they don't come back in. The last thing you want to do is to allow those negative thoughts and feelings to take root in your mind and create the harm they are intended to create. Therefore, create a barrier that keeps unwanted and foreign thoughts and feelings out of your heart and mind. This will enable you to entertain only those thoughts and feelings that bring happiness, peace of mind, and more importantly, health and wellbeing.

Another way to establish emotional boundaries is to determine what is acceptable and what is not. For example, any thought or feeling that makes you feel better about yourself should be welcomed, no matter where it comes from. Alternatively, any thought or feeling that undermines your confidence or sense of self-worth should be rejected, even when you are the author of such thoughts. By taking control of the nature of the thoughts and feelings allowed to stay in your mind, you take control over the nature of your mind itself. This will allow you to replace the harmful influences of past mindsets, mostly created by your emotionally immature parents, with a mindset full of confidence, love, and hope.

The trick to achieving this goal is to contemplate each thought and feeling you have and decide whether to keep it or kick it out. If it is harmful, mentally envision yourself kicking it out of your home. Alternatively, if it is positive in nature envision inviting it in and making it a welcome guest in your house. As you begin to fill your mind with happy, positive thoughts and emotions while removing all unwanted negativity your entire sense of self will be transformed, replacing the negative images created by your parents with positive, inspired images that will give you the power to pursue a life of happiness, fulfillment, and love.

4. Exercise self-care

No doubt most people reading this book will already be familiar with the old axiom "An ounce of prevention is worth a pound of cure." While this is often associated with the maintenance of one's physical health and wellbeing, the fact is that it holds equally true to a person's emotional health and wellbeing. What makes this particularly important is that having put in the time and effort to achieve inner-healing, the last thing you want to do is allow negativity to return to your heart and mind and undo all the progress you have made. Therefore, once you have gained control of your thoughts and feelings, the next step is to ensure you maintain that control by exercising self-care.

One of the most important elements of self-care is to avoid exposure to highly negative people. This can include your emotionally immature parents, but it can also include any other person who is overly negative in nature. Anyone who is given to criticism, self-doubt, hostility, or any other similar negative emotion or mindset can be very dangerous to your emotional wellbeing. The bottom line is that even though you are in the stages of self-healing, you can still be vulnerable to the negative influences of the past, or any that stir them up. Therefore, any time you hear people talking in a negative way, such as belittling someone, criticizing others, or just complaining about life in general, the best thing you can do is to walk away from them and avoid their negative energy. You don't have to interrupt them or ask them to be more positive, simply walk away, and protect yourself from their influence.

Another important form of self-care is to control your own emotional reaction to events and people. It can be all too easy to get angry or frustrated when things don't go according to plan, but that reaction can lead to a negative mindset that can have long-lasting repercussions. The more frustrated you become, the more critical you will become with life in general, leading to you developing a negative mindset that robs you of the happiness and love you desire. Therefore, any time you feel yourself reacting in a negative way it is vital that you become aware of yourself and take control of your thoughts, words, and actions so that they don't take control of you. Tricks like counting to ten when you feel your blood start to boil can make all the difference between reacting in a volatile way that you later regret as opposed to responding in a mature, positive way that keeps things going in the right direction. In the end, taking control over your own thoughts and feelings is just as important, if not more so, than any other step in the inner-healing process.

Finally, there is the element of self-care that tells you to let other people share the burden. This can come in many forms, including finding a mentor, getting counseling, or just simply making friends. At the end of the day, life is hard enough when you have the love and support of others. Anyone who tries to make it through life all alone only makes the journey that much harder. The problem with children of emotionally immature parents is that they have become accustomed to not having the emotional support most others have. This usually means that they never allow themselves to trust others enough to let them help share life's burdens.

The best thing you can do for yourself is to overcome this trust issue and begin to let others into your life. This will provide you with the mental and emotional support necessary to live a happy and healthy life. Whether you choose to make friends that you can spend time with and talk about life with, or you choose to seek direction through a mentor or counselor, the important thing is to find people who you can talk to about your fears, problems, hopes, and dreams. Not only can such people provide helpful advice when you are facing problems, but they can also ensure that you will never have to face another problem all alone ever again. Simply having someone to proverbially watch your back can make all the difference when it comes to overcoming difficult situations in life.

CHAPTER 7

How to Practice Self-care and Unlock Your Potential

Anyone who has ever suffered a serious physical injury will know the importance of daily therapy with regard to rehabilitation. When an individual practices daily exercises they are able to recover from their physical trauma more quickly and more completely than someone who fails to put in regular and meaningful effort. The very same principle holds true in the case of emotional trauma and injury. In order to make a thorough and timely recovery from the injuries inflicted by emotionally immature parents, a person needs to practice self-care on a daily basis. Such a practice will enable you to eliminate all negative energy from your heart and mind, thereby unlocking your potential to live a life full of happiness, meaning, and fulfillment.

This chapter will reveal seven self-care techniques, along with the unique benefits each has to offer. Whether you choose to practice one technique or several, the most important thing is to get into the right mindset. You need to recognize that these techniques are designed to allow you to address your negative thoughts and feelings and push them out of your heart and mind. Therefore, only engage in these practices when you have the time, the space, and most importantly, the privacy you need to get the best results. Eventually, the results of these exercises will begin to show, and you will find that you have less and less negativity to rid yourself of. This will let you know that you are on the right path, the one that will provide you with the inner peace and happiness you deserve. The seven most effective self-care techniques are as follows:

1. **Journaling**

Few things in life are considered as powerful as the written word. The axiom "The pen is mightier than the sword" demonstrates just how powerful the written word can be. One reason for this is that a person spends a great deal more time contemplating their thoughts and choosing their words when writing than they do when speaking. As a result, they tend to be more honest about their thoughts and feelings, digging deeper than they might if they were simply having a conversation with someone. This act of reflection can go a long way to discovering childhood wounds that continue to cause problems in adult life. Once these wounds are discovered, the process of healing them can begin, thereby bringing health and wellbeing to your heart, mind and overall life in general.

Journaling is an excellent way to conduct this in-depth soul searching. On the one hand, it causes you to sit down and really contemplate your heart and mind. This will enable you to see the true face of the things that haunt you and thus allow you to begin to rid yourself of those demons once and for all. Additionally, the very act of writing down your discoveries can serve as an exorcism of sorts, a means by which you transfer the harmful thoughts and feelings from your mind onto paper where they won't be able to hurt you anymore.

Another benefit to journaling is that it is totally private. This allows you to share your deepest and darkest secrets, fears and memories without consequence. The chances are you won't be so open in a verbal conversation with others. Although such conversations can be helpful in many ways, most people are afraid of how others will perceive them if they reveal their deepest traumas. However, since no one is listening to or reading the words you write in your journal you can release even the most horrible thoughts, feelings or memories from your conscience. At first, it may be difficult to be so open and honest about your inner-demons, however as you become familiar with writing in your journal, you will find that you will become more honest and open, and thus rid yourself of the pain that lurks deep within you.

Finally, journaling can also be a useful tool for keeping track of your progress. While your initial writings may be scattered and full of hatred, fear and anger, later writings will reflect a person who is more self-assured, happier, and who has a greater sense of inner peace. When you take the time to compare your early entries with later ones you will see the evolution that your life has gone through, one that leads you from a victim of emotionally immature parents to someone who is confident, driven and full of self-love and respect. This will give you a huge sense of accomplishment, which will only increase all of your positive thoughts and feelings.

2. Meditation

Sometimes a person's mind is so chaotic that it is all but impossible to gain positive control over all of the thoughts and feelings swirling around within. One time tested and proven way to fix this situation is the practice of meditation. The earliest teachings regarding mediation even refer to what is known as the "monkey mind", the state of mental chaos that keeps a person from becoming truly self-aware. Overcoming this monkey mind was one of the main purposes of meditation in the first place. Therefore, if you find that you can't sort out your thoughts and feelings enough to engage in self-care techniques such as journaling you may want to begin practicing meditation in order to achieve clarity in your heart and mind.

There are numerous forms of meditation, each with a unique practice and unique benefits. Since no single form is completely right or wrong it is important that you try out a few different forms in order to determine which one is right for you. A good one to start with is what is known as progressive relaxation or body scan meditation. This is the meditation that allows you to discover tension and anxiety within your body and release it by relaxing the various muscles adversely affected. The first step is to find a quiet place where you won't be disturbed by any person or distraction. Next, sit in a comfortable but upright position and close your eyes. Begin to regulate your breathing so that you are taking slow, deep breaths that are relaxing in nature. You want to start with one end of your body, usually your feet, and focus on how that part feels. Consciously relax your feet and ankles, visualizing a wave of warm and soothing energy enveloping the area. Next, move to your legs and repeat the process. Eventually, you will reach the top of your body, releasing the tension from your neck and head. This form of meditation allows you to both release anxiety from your body as well as develop the ability to focus your mind on one thing at a time. This is why it is a good place to start.

The second form of mediation that can prove useful is known as mindfulness meditation. Unlike most other forms of mediation, this one can be practiced anywhere at all, regardless of noise, distraction and the like. The point of this form of meditation is to develop mindfulness of the present moment. This helps the practitioner break free from the habit of fixating on the past or the future and filling their mind with unnecessary stress and anxiety. The steps for mindfulness meditation are very straightforward. Any time you find yourself fixating on the past or the future simply become aware of where you are. Whether you are in the car, in the grocery store or in the shower, it doesn't matter. Start paying attention to the people and things around you, noticing details about such things as colors, textures and smells. If you are in a public place, start looking at different people, noticing their clothes, their hairstyle, and any other detail that can be noticed in an instant. Once you notice a detail, move on to another person or object and take in any details from that. The goal is to become wholly focused on the people and objects around you, thereby becoming mindful of where you are in the present moment. This will help you to escape the negative act of reliving the past and filling your mind with fear and anger that will only keep you from appreciating the wonderful things within your current life.

Finally, there is a form of meditation known as loving-kindness meditation. This is the practice of opening your heart and mind to the positive energies that surround you, while also developing the habit of sending positive, loving thoughts to the people and things in your life. Like most other forms of meditation, this one should be practiced in a quiet place free from noise or distraction. Sitting in a comfortable yet upright position, you should close your eyes and begin to breathe in a relaxed, regulated way. Next, begin to visualize different things or people in your life, one at a time, and generate a positive response to that image. You should start with things that genuinely bring you pleasure as it is easier to feel good about those things than people who cause you pain. Thus, if you have a cat, dog, or other significant animal companions start with them. Feel love and warmth toward that creature and send out the message that you love them and accept them for who they are. Repeat this process, building your sense of love and compassion until you can comfortably envision people who have caused you pain and harm, such as emotionally immature parents. Visualize your parents and feel love and forgiveness for them. Send them the message that you forgive them for the pain they have caused and that you love them in spite of everything. This will enable you to let go of the events that generate pain and suffering in your mind long after such events have passed.

3. Visualization

Once you have gained control over the content of your heart and mind, you can begin to practice the technique of visualization. This practice is commonly used by some of the most successful people in life, and it has many popular forms, including the well-known Law of Attraction. Basically, visualization is the process of turning dreams into reality. Few techniques of self-care can cure a person of past trauma and pain, quite like the ability to create and live the life of their dreams. Fortunately, although this process requires a fair amount of time and effort, it is, in fact, very easy and straightforward in nature.

The first step in visualization is to choose a goal. This goal can be anything at all, including getting your dream job, finding your dream home, or even meeting your dream partner. Nothing is too big or too small for this process. As such, you might choose to visualize losing ten or even five pounds, getting a raise at work or increasing your workout regimen by five or ten percent. Sometimes starting with smaller, more achievable goals is the way to go as it allows you to develop your visualization skills in a modest yet measurable way.

Once you have your goal in mind clearly visualize what that goal is. You don't have to figure out how to achieve it. You only have to picture it in your mind. Whether it's the perfect job, weight loss, or the person of your dreams, begin to fill your heart and mind with the image of your dream and focus completely on it. See your dream in as much detail as possible, such as the numbers on the scale, the physical features of your dream person, or the environment of your dream job. The important thing is to make the image as real and detailed as possible.

The next step is to add yourself to the picture. See yourself standing on the scale, seeing your target weight for the first time. Go a step further and see yourself wearing the clothes you can fit into when you hit that target weight. Alternatively, see yourself interacting with your dream person. Visualize having a wonderful conversation over lunch or painting the town in an evening of fun and romance. No matter what your dream is, see yourself as an active part of that dream, as though you were watching a movie of what your life will look like when you achieve your life's ambition.

Finally, feel gratitude for achieving your dream. Even if you haven't actually realized it yet begin to feel as though you have. One of the little known secrets shared by successful people is that when you align your thoughts and feelings, you unlock your true potential. Therefore, it isn't enough to simply imagine the life of your dreams; you need to feel it in the very core of your being. Once your mind and heart are unified, you will discover the opportunities that will lead to you achieving those things you desire most, and thus turning your dreams into reality!

4. Yoga

Just as uniting your thoughts and feelings can create powerful results, so too, uniting your body and mind can have a similarly powerful outcome. One of the most common and effective techniques for uniting your body and mind is the practice of yoga. This practice will enable you to explore your innermost thoughts and feelings while releasing stress and tension in your body through a wide array of stretches and poses designed to increase your overall sense of wellbeing. Furthermore, you can choose to practice yoga alone in the comfort and privacy of your home, or you can choose to practice it with others, thereby surrounding yourself with the positive energy of like-minded individuals who are seeking health, happiness and a better life.

The first step to practicing yoga is to get proper instruction. While yoga is a perfectly safe form of exercise when practiced properly, you don't want to risk injury as the result of mistakes or trying positions you aren't ready for. Therefore, you might want to start practicing under the supervision of a licensed professional who can guide you in the beginning stages of your yoga practice. Afterward, you can acquire instructional videos that will enable you to perform any level of yoga on your own.

One of the main focuses of yoga is breathing. This serves two main functions. First, it causes the practitioner to become aware of the present moment. When you focus on your breathing, you lose the ability to let your mind drift to painful childhood memories or stressful thoughts of the future. This helps you pay attention to your posture while practicing yoga, which ensures you stay safe and get the best results possible. The second reason for focusing on your breathing is to help relax your body. This enables you to stretch and move more freely as your muscles aren't tight and tense. Additionally, this also helps to reduce any strain or injury that tense or tight muscles might cause when practicing some of the more advanced poses. Therefore, whether you practice with others or alone, it is vital that you take your breathing seriously, as it is perhaps the most important element of yoga.

The act of focusing your mind, and thus clearing it of negative thoughts and emotions, coupled with the act of releasing stress and tension from your body through stretches and poses makes yoga one of the most comprehensive self-care techniques with regard to healing your body and mind of the traumas of your past. As you develop your ability to focus your mind, you will achieve greater levels of mental peace and tranquility. These will allow you to let go of pain and suffering and become the happy, loving person you truly are. Furthermore, by developing a connection with your body, you can increase your sense of self-love and appreciation, thereby replacing any negative self-images from the past with a positive sense of self that will improve every area of your life.

5. Art therapy

While the pen might be mightier than the sword, it is claimed that a picture is worth a thousand words. Therefore, some might argue that art, not writing, is truly the most powerful form of communication and expression. That said, there are many places that utilize what is known as art therapy to help a person cope with the traumas of their past and rid themselves of their inner demons once and for all. Although art therapy can produce best results when done under the supervision and direction of a licensed professional the fact is that it can produce significant and measurable changes even when practiced alone in the safety and security of your own home. Therefore, if you feel the need to express your thoughts and feelings through something other than meditation or exercise, art therapy might be the self-care technique for you.

Psychologists often use paintings and drawings to determine a person's inner state of mind. In fact, depression, anger, and other such emotions can be divined in the works of the masters such as Van Gogh, Monet, and others. While the artist may not have intended for their feelings to seep through into their works, it is an inevitable occurrence. This means that the acts of painting and drawing are perfect techniques for discovering and expressing your inner thoughts and feelings. Fortunately, you don't have to be an accomplished artist in order for art to help you release your negative emotions, rather you just have to be able to follow your inspiration and use the shapes, colors, and textures that speak to you in the moment. The bottom line is that expressing emotions through art is a highly effective way to release fear, anger, and other emotions that words alone may not be able to capture. When used as a form of therapy, most people claim a sense of release after their art session. Keeping a sketchpad and a pencil on hand may be all that it takes to release your pent up frustrations and restore your mind to a calm and serene state once again.

Music is another highly effective form of art therapy. Again, you don't even have to be able to play a musical instrument in order to gain the results from this form of expression. All you need to do is to be able to use an instrument to make the noises that match your mood. Banging on low piano keys to express dark, brooding emotions can go a long way to releasing those emotions into the Universe, thereby clearing your heart and mind. Alternatively, you might want to beat on a drum to release anger and frustration. Drumming ceremonies are a common practice within many traditions, and using them to exorcise demons, and mental ailments are something that goes back hundreds and even thousands of years. The key is to express your thoughts and emotions using the tones and rhythms that best represent them. In essence, you are using the musical instrument as the mouthpiece of your soul.

Finally, for those who prefer a more physical experience, there is the art therapy technique of interpretive dance. This is when a person moves their body in a way to express a certain emotion or mood or to tell a story to those watching. Fortunately, you don't have to dance in front of an audience to get the job done. Instead, you just have to let your body begin to move in a way that allows you to express your pain and suffering. Eventually, through the movement and the energy, you use, you will feel a sense of release, as though your negative energy has all been spent in your dance exercise. You can use music that matches your mood to inspire your dance moves, or you can dance to silence, letting your thoughts and feelings do the talking.

6. **Developing mindfulness**

This chapter has already discussed the technique of mindfulness meditation and the results it can have on improving your overall state of mind. Such mindfulness can be achieved without the process of meditation, something good for those who feel too undisciplined for meditation or who want to practice something free of religious or spiritual overtones. Developing mindfulness is something that anyone can do no matter where they are or what activities they are involved in. The methods are similar to mindfulness meditation but somewhat more varied.

One method for developing mindfulness is to pay extra attention to your surroundings. Unlike mindfulness meditation, however, you don't have to move from one thing to another in quick succession. Instead, you can linger on a particular thing for as long as you like. The reason you would do this would be to gain a deeper understanding of why something triggers an emotional response within. For example, if you noticed a smell that you found pleasant, you could take the time to ask yourself why it affects you that way. Ask yourself if it reminds you of something pleasant, or if you just prefer smells that fall into certain categories. This is an excellent way to better understand who you are and the way that your surroundings impact your thoughts and feelings. You might do the same thing with something you find visually pleasing, such as a work of art or even a person's outfit. The important thing is to become wholly aware of a particular thing and how that thing influences you.

Another technique for developing mindfulness is to regularly take stock of how you are feeling. All too often, people simply go through their day, never taking the time to consider their thoughts or feelings. As a result, those thoughts and feelings can influence the decisions they make without them even realizing it. To regain control of your decision-making paradigm, it is vital that you maintain a constant awareness over your general state of being. At random times ask yourself how you are feeling. When you discover the answer, take it a step further and ask yourself, "Why?" This is how you develop not only mindfulness over your thoughts and feelings, but also mindfulness over the triggers that influence those thoughts and feelings. When you discover the cause of your state of mind, you can better understand yourself and the dynamics of your inner-self. This can help you to be aware of influences that might have a negative impact on your mindset, and thus avoid them in order to maintain a positive state of mind. Alternatively, it can also help you to identify those things that bring you happiness so that you can be more open to them and the healthy, happy influences they provide.

Finally, there is the aspect of being aware of not just where you are, but of where you *aren't*. This means that when you find yourself fixating on the past, you can remind yourself that you aren't that helpless child anymore and that your parents can't cause you pain and suffering anymore. By reminding yourself that you are no longer in your past, you can reduce and even eliminate the emotional effects of past traumas, leaving them far behind where they belong. You can take it a step further and focus on a pleasant aspect of your current life. This can be your job, your friends, or even your cat. When you focus on the happy aspects of your present, you prevent the past from dictating your life, and thus, you give yourself the opportunity to replace pain and suffering with joy, gratitude, and love.

7. Cognitive-behavioral therapy

Some physical conditions, such as a cough or a cold, can be treated by the individual with over the counter meds that are readily available. However, some physical conditions, such as broken bones, pneumonia, or cancer, cannot be treated the same way. Instead, they require the attention of professional doctors, as well as drugs and other medicines not available to the average person. Emotional conditions act in the exact same way. While some people are able to treat and overcome their mental and emotional suffering on their own with basic tools readily available, other people need the help of professionals due to the complexity and severity of their condition. In the event that the previously discussed forms of self-care do not produce measurable results, it may be necessary for you to seek help by a qualified and licensed professional. One form of treatment that helps to heal emotional and mental trauma is known as Cognitive Behavioral Therapy or CBT for short. When all else fails, this may be the best direction to take in order to regain control of your life and heal the pain and suffering from your past.

In short, CBT is the process of examining irrational behaviors and thoughts within people and seeking to replace them with thoughts and behaviors of a more rational nature. The first step to achieving this goal is to take an irrational thought and reveal the flaws within it. For example, a person may feel that everyone is watching them and criticizing what they do. Needless to say, that is never the case, no matter who you are. Thus the therapist will make the individual examine this thought process and see that it simply doesn't hold true. They may first trace this mindset back to rejecting parents who constantly berated and criticized the individual, thereby determining its origin. Next, they may provide proof that other people aren't criticizing them. In a group session, this could take the form of asking the other people to close their eyes and describe the individual. The lack of accurate descriptions would prove a lack of interest in the individual by other people, thus debunking the notion that everyone was paying close attention to them.

This same process can be used to examine behaviors, beliefs and other thoughts that are usually the result of a traumatic childhood in which a person's emotional and mental development were stunted or affected in a way so as to distort their view of other people, events and life in general. It has been an effective tool in overcoming such things as anger issues, low self-esteem, eating disorders, and other behaviors that are harmful either to the person or to society in general. As this technique often involves a group setting, it can take a great deal of time and effort before an individual feels comfortable enough to open up in order to begin changing their lives for the better. However, since they will be able to hear other people discuss their problems, it can be a hugely positive experience, one that assures the individual that they are not alone in their pain and suffering.

In the end, the goal of CBT is to help a person gain control of their thoughts, beliefs, and emotional responses to life. The lesson is that while an individual can't control the events around them, they can control how they respond to those events. In essence, CBT is a way to develop positive coping skills within a person who lacked proper guidance as a child. Studies conducted show that as a result of this approach, CBT can be as effective as or more effective than other more conventional treatments when treating people with addiction and substance abuse. This is because the harmful behaviors were revealed as not actually providing the relief they promised. Thus, the belief in those behaviors was eliminated, and the behaviors themselves became replaced with healthier ones for the individual and everyone else concerned.

CBT has also been found to be as effective as other conventional treatments for other conditions such as bipolar disorder, anxiety disorders, and anger management issues. In each case, the results were equal to treatments such as conventional psychoanalysis, intervention therapies, and even the use of certain medications. However, perhaps the greatest discovery was that CBT, when used in conjunction with other treatment methods, provided enhanced results that reduced recovery time as well as the likelihood of relapse. Subsequently, if your emotional needs require results that self-care alone cannot provide, you might want to find a CBT professional in your area and integrate that technique with the other methods discussed in this book.

CHAPTER 8

How to Heal the Relationships with Your Parents

When it comes to healing emotional wounds, few things are as important as a strong sense of closure. Such closure enables a person to draw a line in their life, leaving the past on one side of the line and starting a new life on the other. Only when you can leave the past behind you can you effectively move on and begin to live the life you want. Until then, memories, regrets, and pains from the past will continue to haunt your mind, influencing, and even controlling your life in highly negative ways. One of the best ways to find closure with regards to a traumatic childhood is to sit down and have a heart-to-heart conversation with your emotionally immature parents.

This conversation can be one of the hardest things you will ever do, but it can also turn out to be one of the most beneficial things you can do in terms of bringing about positive change in your life. Furthermore, such a conversation may actually improve the relationship you have with your parents, thus providing further comfort from the traumas of your past. That said, it is absolutely vital that you don't approach this conversation half-heartedly. Instead, you need to make sure that every element of the event is carefully planned out so that you give yourself the best chance of achieving the results you desire. This chapter will reveal some of the most important elements with regard to structuring, planning, and initiating this all-important conversation.

1. **Choosing the right place for the conversation**

The first thing you need to do when planning to have your heart-to-heart conversation is to choose the location for the conversation to take place. In some ways, this can be seen as the most important step, as choosing the wrong location can cause things to fall apart even before they get started.

Therefore, you should spend your time and energy finding the right place before you start thinking about the things you want to say.

An easy mistake to make is to choose a location that is comfortable for you but unfamiliar to your parents. Many people think that by having their conversation in a place where they feel in charge, they will gain the upper hand, thereby enabling them to be in control of the situation. Thus, they invite their parents over to their home or some similar environment in an attempt to undermine the controlling nature of their parents and give them the proverbial home-field advantage. Unfortunately, this strategy backfires almost every time. The simple truth is that emotionally immature people become defensive when they are out of their comfort zone, and parents are no exception to this. Therefore, if you try to use the home-field advantage, you will only cause your parents to shut off right from the start, making your conversation ineffective and your time and effort wasted.

An equally bad mistake is to hold the conversation in your parents' home or some equally comfortable environment in which they feel in control. This will only make your efforts more difficult as your parents will draw strength from their surroundings, thus becoming more and more overwhelming as the conversation develops. Therefore, never, ever think that your determination and resolve will prove strong enough to overcome such a disadvantage. Instead, choose to have your conversation in a completely neutral place, somewhere that neither party gains an advantage or a disadvantage from. This will prevent both you and your parents from becoming overly defensive or overly aggressive during the course of the encounter.

Public places such as restaurants or shopping malls can be used to create a neutral, safe environment for your conversation. However, these places have certain drawbacks. The other people in your close proximity can cause you to become self-conscious, thereby distracting your attention from the mission at hand. This can cause you to avoid saying things you really want to say, or from expressing your emotions fully. Therefore, a better choice is somewhere neutral and fairly private, such as a park, the beach, or someplace where you can talk and act freely without feeling as though you are on display. Furthermore, such a place will allow either party to leave suddenly, unlike a restaurant where you will have to finish eating and pay the check before you can depart.

2. Starting the conversation right

Once you have chosen the location for your conversation, the next step is to come up with the content of the conversation itself. Just as the wrong location can destroy any hope of a successful outcome, so too, starting the conversation on the wrong foot can result in defeat even before the "battle" gets underway. The most important thing in starting your conversation is to focus on the future rather than the present. If you start by saying how traumatized you were as a child, you create an atmosphere of judgment and condemnation, one that will result in a defensive posture by any person, let alone emotionally immature parents. Therefore, begin the conversation by stating your intention, namely that you want your relationship with your parents to be better than what it currently is.

Establishing a goal that has both parties' best interests at heart is a sure way of demonstrating peaceful and benevolent intentions, ones that your parents can be receptive to. The key is to get your parents to open up as the conversation develops, and assuring them that your goals are positive can help to get them to open up right at the start. Furthermore, by telling your parents that you want your relationship to improve, you give them the opportunity to present any grievances or desires on their part. Just because they are emotionally immature doesn't mean that they are wrong on every single subject. The fact is that you might need to recognize your own flaws with regard to your side of the relationship. In the end, this conversation can help lead to growth on both sides, not just on the side of your parents.

3. How to avoid triggering a blow-up

Getting things off to the right start is only half the battle. The other half is making sure that things stay on track and don't get derailed as a result of saying something that triggers the dreaded all-powerful blow up that will end your conversation instantly and permanently. Subsequently, it is vital that you avoid getting drawn into a debate or an argument of any sort. Instead, allow your parents to have their say without rejecting or criticizing their opinions. Even if their opinions or statements are completely unfair, untrue, or overly hostile, it is critical that you don't allow the conversation to devolve into an argument. Once an argument takes shape, your chances of achieving closure, let alone a better relationship with your parents, are completely shot.

Remember, you are likely to only get one chance to make this conversation work. Therefore, it is critical that you do everything you can to ensure that it achieves your goals the first time around.

A good plan for avoiding an argument is to keep tabs on your emotional state. Understand, this conversation isn't going to be a pleasant experience. Instead, it is going to be very stressful, resulting in your nerves being frayed even before you arrive at your chosen location. Therefore, it is vital that you use every tool you have with regards to keeping your emotions in check. The last thing you need to do is to lose your head, react in a hostile and irrational manner, and thus undermine your chances of success. Keep a cool head, no matter what your parents say. You may need to count to five, ten or even one hundred in order to keep a calm demeanor and avoid from reacting to harmful statements from your parents. However, such efforts will be worthwhile if they help you to achieve your desired results.

Another good strategy is to remind yourself of any words, facial expressions, or other "ticks" that might engender an emotionally charged response from your parents. It can be all too easy to roll your eyes when someone says something completely irrational. Such an expression might be all that is needed to trigger a blow-up, and thus bring your conversation to a close. Therefore, in order to give yourself the best chance of success, you should rehearse your conversation in front of a mirror, imagining every possible response from your parents. Practice keeping a calm and composed demeanor as you respond to even the worst things your parents could say. You might even have a friend sit in for your parents, thereby creating responses you might be unprepared for. This will help you to develop the stage presence necessary to keep things under control no matter how volatile emotions might become.

4. How to stay true to yourself

Even with the most carefully planned setting, introduction, and conversation structure, there can still be several dangers lurking in the shadows that can undermine all of your efforts and intentions. One such danger is in losing yourself to the momentum of the moment. Needless to say, a conversation of this magnitude with emotionally immature parents is going to be unpredictable at best. The amount of push-back and aggression by parents can be enough to scramble the mind of even the best-prepared person. Emotionally immature parents will want to control the tone and nature of every conversation they have, and this one will be no exception. Therefore, it is vital that you take extra precautions in order to ensure that you stay true to yourself and your goals no matter what your parents try to do.

A good way to stay true to yourself all throughout the conversation is to write down the points that you want to cover. You don't need to write down the entire conversation you want to have, word for word, as though it were a script. Instead, you just need to have a list of important topics that you feel need to be addressed and hopefully resolved. It can be all too easy to imagine that you couldn't possibly lose track of your thoughts and intentions since you've virtually spent your whole life contemplating them. However, the impact emotionally immature parents can have on your mind should never be underestimated. Once such parents get on a tangent, it can change the course of a conversation dramatically, and only the best-prepared person will have any chance to regain control and get things back on track. This is where having a list of topics will prevent you from losing yourself to the direction and momentum of an emotionally charged attempt by your parents to hijack the conversation and turn the course of the narrative in their favor.

Equally as important as keeping track of your thoughts is having the right mindset for this highly challenging conversation. It is vital that you remain as emotionally detached from the situation in order to prevent your parents from being able to manipulate you and the situation with the tricks and underhanded tactics they have used to control you your entire life. One way to achieve this state of detachment is to think of yourself as an outsider weighing in on both parties, acting as a mediator of sorts. This mindset will keep you from taking any harsh words personally, and thus help you to keep a clear mind no matter what your parents do or say. Pretend that you are a lawyer trying to settle a dispute, and that you have nothing to lose or gain personally in the matter. When you remove the notion of winning or losing, you remove the fear and anxiety from the situation, enabling you to act with tact, grace, and most importantly, dignity.

5. How to effectively set boundaries

Finally, there is the aspect of setting effective emotional boundaries. These boundaries act as the rules of engagement, so to speak, ensuring a level playing field for all participants. Many people make the mistake of using emotional boundaries as a sort of emergency escape, one that allows them to cut and run when things get too heated or too much to handle. While this may sound like a good plan, it can have the undesired effect of giving a person the opportunity to quit before they achieve their goals. In the end, this conversation is designed to benefit you. Therefore you want to stay in it until the end at almost all costs. However, it is vital that you protect yourself from the unnecessary harm and trauma that emotionally immature parents could try to inflict in such circumstances.

Some of the boundaries to put in place might include such things as fixating on the past, playing the "blame game", and becoming overly hostile, both in the tone as well as the content of what is said. The only way that your conversation can bear positive and lasting results is if it is done in a decent and fair way. Therefore, anything that undermines fairness and decency can be included in boundaries set for the conversation. You can choose to discuss these boundaries at the start, although that can have the undesired result in creating a hostile tone for the event. As such, it is recommended that you address infractions as they occur, noting how they are unhealthy for the intention of improving relations and thus should be avoided.

In addition to setting boundaries for the conversation itself, you can also set boundaries regarding the role your parents play in your life from this point on. Such things as controlling attitudes, interference in personal affairs, emotional abuse, and the like can be established as actions that won't be tolerated in the future. Needless to say, you might want to rephrase the items on your list in order to make the list sound less critical and damming in nature. You might even choose to use specific examples of behavior you don't want repeated, thereby avoiding the use of titles and tags that can be misconstrued either innocently or for sinister reasons. The important thing is to establish a sense of fair play regarding the relationship you hope to have with your parents. It may take a while for these new rules to take hold, but if you enforce them effectively, you should see them begin to influence your relationship in a positive way. Ways you might enforce your chosen rules can include hanging up when your parents shout over the phone, sending your parents home when they invade your space, or any similar measure to instantly end misbehavior. In the end, it's all about preventing your parents from controlling your life in a negative way, therefore identifying and rejecting negative behavior are two absolutely vital steps toward achieving that goal.

CHAPTER 9

How to Let Go of a Toxic Relationship

History, they say, tends to repeat itself. This is especially true when valuable lessons go unlearned, leaving a person or group of people to repeat the same mistakes over and over again, resulting in the same pain and suffering each and every time. The same dangerous cycle occurs in the lives of many children of emotionally immature parents. Subsequently, even when an individual is safely away from the reach of their parents, they tend to gravitate to other toxic relationships. Such toxic relationships seem normal to those who remain stuck in their past, however when a person chooses to let go of their past and begin the road to recovery they start to see how toxic in nature many of their other relationships actually are. This results in them needing to try and fix those relationships as well as the relationship they have with their parents.

Unfortunately, not all relationships are fixable. Many are doomed to remain in a highly toxic state, no matter how much time and effort is put into changing things for the better. In these cases the individual needs to decide whether they wish to remain in a relationship that will always be toxic or whether they wish to leave the relationship behind, thereby focusing on their own emotional health and overall wellbeing. This chapter will discuss the various ways in which to leave a relationship that simply cannot be salvaged, including the ultimate relationship between a person and their parents. The three main issues regarding toxic relationships include the following:

1. **What is a toxic relationship**

A toxic relationship is exactly what the name implies. It is a relationship that causes you significant harm. Just as a toxic plant can make a person seriously sick if they ingest it, so too, toxic relationships significantly harm a person in emotional, psychological, and even physical ways. Any relationship that causes fear, depression, pain, and suffering is, by definition, toxic. Perhaps the most important thing to remember is that the more intimate the relationship is, the more harmful it can become. Therefore, recognizing and dealing with such relationships is absolutely vital for anyone who wants to put emotional abuse behind them once and for all and begin living the happy, loving life they truly deserve.

2. How to recognize when a relationship is toxic

Toxic relationships can take many forms; as such, there are many different signs that can help you to recognize when a relationship is toxic. These forms run the full range from passive to passive-aggressive to outright aggressive. They include all forms of abuse, including psychological, emotional, and even physical. Most toxic relationships combine two or more signs, meaning that each toxic relationship is as unique as the people it involves. The important thing is to be able to recognize the signs of a toxic relationship in order to protect yourself from the dangers it poses. Common signs of a toxic relationship are as follows:

- **The relationship is one-sided.** One of the most common characteristics of a toxic relationship is that one person puts in all the time and effort to make the relationship work. The other person, in contrast, never contributes to the wellbeing of the relationship. Instead, they enjoy all the benefits without having to put in any of the work.

- **You constantly feel nervous.** It's one thing to feel nervous around a boss or some other form of a supervisor who has the power to make your life extremely good or extremely bad, depending on how they view your performance. However, that same feeling should never be experienced in a personal relationship, especially an intimate one. Unfortunately, many people live in relationships that feel as though they are being scrutinized every minute of every day, leaving them emotionally drained as a result.

- **There is an ongoing scorecard.** Children of emotionally immature parents are all too familiar with the "points game." This is when your actions either score positive points with your parents or negative points. Good actions will score positive points, while actions that are disappointing or rebellious in nature will score negative points. Even worse, good actions will usually only score a handful of points while bad actions score points by the tens of thousands. If you find yourself in this scenario, you are in a toxic relationship.

- **A lack of privacy.** When no space is sacred, including the text messages on your phone or the contacts list on your social media platforms, your privacy isn't being respected. This is a telltale sign that your partner is highly insecure, and thus that your relationship is in fact, toxic.

- **You are always to blame.** When everything is your fault, even though it isn't, you are in a toxic relationship. This is especially true when the other person is never at fault, and that instead of being wrong, they are merely misunderstood.

- **The other person is dishonest.** If you are in a relationship with someone who lies constantly, you are in a toxic relationship. Honesty is one of the most important elements of any relationship, and when it is lacking, the relationship is doomed to fail.

- **Abuse.** Whether it is psychological, emotional, or physical, abuse is abuse. The bottom line is that if the other person in a relationship is abusive to you, it means that they have no problem with causing you harm. This is about as toxic as it gets.

3. **How to let go of relationships that aren't beneficial to you**

Once you have seen the signs that a relationship is toxic, and every effort to improve the situation has failed, the next step is to let go of the relationship. Only when you free yourself of all sources of abuse and harm can you begin to transform your life completely into one of health, happiness, and love. However, leaving a toxic relationship is not always as easy as simply getting up and walking away. Instead, it requires specific actions to ensure that you leave the relationship in a way that is beneficial to you, and that prevents the pain and suffering from following you into other relationships. The following steps are some of the most effective ways of letting go of toxic relationships in a healthy and self-loving way:

- **Accept the situation.** Most people stay in toxic relationships because they don't allow themselves to accept just how toxic the other person truly is. Additionally, they may be waiting around in the hopes that the other person will eventually change. Only when you recognize the severity of the situation can you give yourself permission to leave the other person.

- **Brace for impact.** The unfortunate truth is that ending a relationship, even a toxic one, will cause you a fair amount of sadness, pain, and even regret. Therefore, you must expect these emotions to occur. Many people see these negative emotions as a sign that they were wrong to end the relationship, causing them to return to the toxic person they yearn to be free of. This is about as far from the truth as possible. These emotions are natural, and should never be read into in such a way. Fortunately, in the case of toxic relationships, these negative emotions will evaporate over relatively quickly, giving way to a sense of freedom, happiness, and general wellbeing.

- **Give yourself time to recover.** The last thing you want to do is fill the gap created by leaving a toxic relationship too quickly. You need to take some time to heal from the harm that the toxic relationship caused. Therefore, once you leave a person, whether it's a friend, partner or even parent, take time to appreciate the relationships you have and the life you have before trying to take on any new relationships. This will also give you a chance to evaluate the toxic nature of the relationship in a way that will allow you to avoid similar relationships in the future.

- **Embrace your worth.** Guilt can follow any break-up, even one from a toxic person. The best way to eliminate and even prevent guilt is to focus on the fact that you deserve better. No one deserves to be in a toxic relationship. That's what makes the relationship toxic in the first place. Even so, it is extremely important that you remind yourself that you deserve to be happy, appreciated, and more importantly, loved. The more you embrace your worth is, the more necessary leaving the relationship will seem, thereby helping to heal any guilt, regret, or shame that might still linger.

- **Surround yourself with positivity.** Once you leave a toxic relationship, it is important to surround yourself with positivity. This can take the form of positive people, places, or events. By surrounding yourself with positivity, you will ensure that all negative residual energy from your relationship evaporates, making way for more positive energy. Thus, fear, shame, and low self-esteem will be replaced by happiness, love, and a greater sense of self-worth. This positive energy will not only serve to heal the wounds of the past; it will also serve to create a better future, one full of rewarding, loving relationships that will complete your life.

- **Keep a journal.** Sometimes the process of recovering from a toxic relationship can be slower and less dramatic than you might expect. This isn't to say that the end result isn't extraordinary. Instead, it means that the path to that result is gradual and subtle rather than sudden and explosive. A good way to recognize the results of even the slowest recovery process is to keep a journal recording your day-to-day life after ending your toxic relationship. You can start by recording how you felt prior to the break-up, and then begin tracking your emotional state each and every day after the break-up. By keeping track of your thoughts and feelings during this time, you can realize just how much progress you are making, even if it is one step at a time, one day at a time. Eventually, all those steps and days will add up, creating a new and exciting life that is free of the pain and suffering of the past.

While letting go of any relationship can be difficult at best and downright traumatizing at worst, it can be especially painful in the case of having to let go of the relationship with your parents. There is something inherent in a person's nature to want to hang on to their parents no matter what, however, some relationships are so toxic that doing so will only lead to the most negative of outcomes. Therefore, when every effort to improve and salvage the relationship has failed, it can become necessary to let go of the relationship you have with your parents. This decision should not be made lightly. Instead, it should be made when no other option remains available. Subsequently, it is vital that you make this decision with complete insight, conviction, and compassion, thereby making it as positive a decision as possible. The following are two main points to consider when tackling this life-changing decision and the consequences it will bring.

1. **When to let go of your parents**

Since your relationship with your parents is not one you can ever truly replace, it is vital that you only let go of it when absolutely necessary. Fortunately, it isn't hard to know when your relationship with your parents is too toxic to salvage. The trick is to read the signs and to give yourself permission when those signs are clear and evident. The following are some of the most common signs that letting go of your parents is the right thing to do:

- **Your efforts to improve your relationship have failed.** The last chapter focused on how to have the all-important conversation with your emotionally immature parents regarding how you want your relationship to evolve. While some parents will respond positively to this conversation. others will not. If your efforts meet with absolute rejection, it is time to sever ties for your own good. Otherwise, you are destined to remain in a toxic relationship for the rest of your life.

- **Their behavior becomes worse over time.** One of the things with toxic people is that they become even more toxic as time progresses. This stands to reason since they only see life through a negative lens, thus the more life they experience, the more negativity they create. As their energy becomes more negative, so too, their behavior will become more toxic. Occasional criticism turns into constant criticism, yelling becomes more common and intense, and the blame game reaches all-new levels, causing you pain and suffering beyond measure. When this becomes the nature of your relationship, it is time to let it go.

- **Your behavior becomes worse.** Many people face the unenviable choice of leaving their parents or becoming exactly like them. If you discover that you are becoming more and more toxic in your interactions with others, much the way that your parents are with you, then it might be time to sever ties in order to free yourself of their negative influence. You will never be your best as long as you allow inferior ways to shape that you are and how you behave. Therefore, if you are becoming more and more like your emotionally immature parents, you need to separate from them as soon as possible.

- **You find yourself living for your parents.** Ordinarily, parents live for their children, not the other way around. However, in the case of emotionally immature parents, it is the children who live for their parents. In many cases, this changes once the child leaves their parents' home; however, in more extreme cases, even that isn't enough. If you find that you are unable to escape the expectations and demands of your parents even though you are a grown adult living on your own or with your own family it might be time to let go of the past.

2. How to let go even if you still love your parents

Some parents are so toxic that they become detestable, making it easier to break free from them and the pain and suffering that they cause. Unfortunately, this isn't the case when you still love the parents you need to break away from. Letting go of parents, you still love can be very painful, so much so that most people never allow themselves to go through with it. However, when toxic parents are ruining your life, it is vital that you leave them behind even if you still love them. The following are some tips on how to end your relationship when you still love your parents, making the process easier and less negative in nature.

- **Don't create blame.** One of the easiest things to do when breaking up with someone is to point out all the bad things that person did and blame them for all of your unhappiness. Needless to say, this only makes the situation worse, causing the other party even more pain and guilt than the breakup alone will cause. Since you still love your parents, you want to spare them as much pain as possible, therefore don't focus on their faults or blame them for the problems in your life.

- **Don't try to convince them of your reasons.** You don't need to prove yourself to your parents. After all, if you were able to get them to see things your way, you wouldn't need to break up with them in the first place. Since you do need to break up with them, don't try to argue your point. This will only lead to arguing and conflict, and that will only make the situation worse. In the end, you want this process to be as smooth and painless as possible, therefore avoid creating a point of debate that will only increase tension and negativity.

- **Focus on your independence.** Rather than focusing on your need to be free from your parents focus instead on your need to be alone. This will shift the "blame" onto you, thereby reducing any guilt or pain for your parents. In the case that you have a family simply state that you need to focus your attention on them and their expectations. This has the added element of focusing on the future instead of the past, thus making it seem like a more positive process overall.

- **Spend time with others who have been in similar situations.** Once you have broken free from your toxic parents, it is important to affirm the correctness of your decision. The best way to do this is to spend time with people who understand what you have gone through. These people will be able to share their experiences with you, helping you to realize you are not alone. Furthermore, they will be able to validate your thoughts and feelings and help you to find your feet when it comes to creating a life of independence, happiness, and purpose.

- **Leave the door open for future restoration.** No one can ever predict the future. Therefore no action taken in the moment should ever be seen as permanent. This applies to ending relationships with those you love. Even though things are impossible to fix now, that doesn't mean they won't be fixable down the road. Who knows? Maybe your parents will have an epiphany that enables them to become less toxic and thus more deserving of being a part of your life. Alternatively, you might become strong enough as an individual to weather the toxic nature of their relationship, thereby enabling you to have a relationship with them without it causing you harm or distress. In any event, leaving the proverbial door unlocked for a future return is always a good way of lessening the negative consequences of breaking up with your parents. It will also alleviate your sadness as you hold onto the hope of a future restoration that will see both sides happy and healthy.

CHAPTER 10

How to Overcome the Effects of Your Upbringing and Become a Good Parent to Your Own Children

One of the most devastating effects of being raised by emotionally immature parents is the gripping fear that you will turn out to be just like them. The idea of becoming your parents and destroying the life of your own child is enough to make many people abstain from having a family of their own. Countless people sacrifice the potential happiness of parenthood in order to ensure that the abusive nature of their parents doesn't continue down the family tree. Fortunately, you don't have to make such a sacrifice in order to keep the effects of your parents' emotional immaturity in the past. Instead, by practicing some basic and effective exercises, you can become a healthy and loving parent, one that provides the joy and security your parents failed to give. This chapter will reveal five practical parenting tips that will help you overcome your past and become the parent you wish you had when you were growing up.

1. Practice Self-care

The first tip to becoming a loving and healthy parent is to practice plenty of self-care. This includes such things as getting plenty of downtime to recharge your batteries, eating right, getting enough sleep, and taking time to appreciate the things you have. By practicing these methods each and every day, you will significantly reduce your stress levels. This, in turn, will enable you to become more mindful, and thus, more in control of your emotions, thoughts, words, and actions.

Another important aspect of self-care is to talk to someone when things become more than you feel you can handle. Whether you choose to talk to a close friend, a family member or even a professional therapist the important thing is that you find someone who will both listen to your concerns and help you to find solutions. The feeling of being alone in any given situation can increase the anxiety of that moment exponentially, making your struggles even greater. However, having someone that you can talk to and ask for advice can make all the difference, thus ensuring that you never get overwhelmed by life and become the emotional wreck your parents were.

2. Give your child time

Once you have your emotional and mental wellbeing taken care of the next step is to help take care of your child's emotional needs. Most children of emotionally immature parents suffered from being neglected for most of their childhood. The best way to heal those wounds is to make sure that you give your child the time they need to feel loved, appreciated, and most importantly, wanted. Spending quality time with your child on a daily basis will ensure that they get the emotional nurturing they need in order to become mentally and emotionally strong as they grow.

Another benefit to spending quality time with your child on a daily basis is the bond that such time creates. The more time you spend with any other person is the closer to that person you become. This applies to your child just as much if not even more so. Therefore, if you want to establish the bond with your child that you never had with your parents make sure you spend regular time with them every day doing something that matters to them as well as to you.

Quality time with a child can come in almost any form, so the important thing is to try several different techniques until you find those that work for you. One common activity is reading. Whether you choose to read a bedtime story or you choose to read something in the middle of the day is up to you. The act of reading will have the same impact no matter when it's done. Not only will this create a loving bond between you and your child, it will also increase your child's mental development, thereby giving them an edge in life when they start school.

Other activities include playing sports, engaging in crafts or artistic activities, or any other practice that will encourage your child to develop their inherent talents. The important thing is to respond to your child rather than force your child to respond to you. Therefore, if you see them playing with a ball, bat, or other piece of sporting equipment, spend your time developing their athletic skills. Alternatively, if they like to draw, paint or engage in another creative activity such as singing or playing music then join them in that activity and establish your bond while helping them to uncover their inner talents.

3. Put yourself in your child's shoes

Growing up is a difficult process, even when you have the best parents in the world. Needless to say, it gets even harder when your parents are emotionally immature. That said, just because you overcome the demons from your past and practice the parenting you wish you had been raised with doesn't mean that your child won't face difficult times throughout their childhood. The best thing you can do in these cases is to put yourself in your child's shoes. This will enable you to better understand your child, and thus offer them the help and support they need. Sometimes they might need time alone in order to work out their thoughts and feelings, while other times they might need you to hold them close and tell them everything is going to be OK. The important thing is to remember that no single remedy cures all ills. Therefore, be attentive to their needs and respond in the way they need you to. This is the essence of developing parent-child empathy.

Another benefit to developing parent-child empathy is that it will serve to heal the emotional wounds from your childhood. By stepping into your child's shoes, and sharing in their pain and struggles, you provide the care and compassion that you lacked as a child. As you give that care and compassion to your child, you, in turn, give it to your inner child, thereby relieving it of its feeling of abandonment. In the end, the effort you put into relating to your child and providing the love and support they need becomes self-serving in a way as you benefit as much from the love you give as they do. Even better, when they show their gratitude for your love and empathy, it will go a long way to proving that you have overcome your past and become your very best.

4. Avoid using authoritarian behavior

Needless to say, there will be times when your child and you don't see eye to eye on a subject, but you know that your decision must stand as it is in their best interest. The chances are any time such an event took place when you were growing up, your parents played the dictator card, reminding you that you lived in their house, and that meant you followed their rules. While this approach can end an argument quickly, it can also end any chances of a parent forming a loving and lasting bond with their child. Therefore, if you want to be the best possible parent for your child, you have to take that dictator card out of your pack and tear it up. There are always better ways to solve the situation.

One way to solve the situation is to discuss things with your child as though they actually are capable of understanding complex ideas. The important thing is to never treat your child like an imbecile. Being young isn't the same as being stupid. If you take the time to explain things in simple terms, you just might get through to your child and make them realize your perspective. This can help them to make better decisions the next time a similar situation presents itself.

Unfortunately, there will be times when discussing the matter won't get the job done. In this case, you may have to put the proverbial foot down and take charge of the situation. However, this doesn't mean that you have to be mean about it. You can be loving and caring as you drag your child away from making a bad decision. By avoiding authoritarian behavior, you become more consistent in your child's mind. They know they can trust you even when you are preventing them from having their own way. This ensures that they will never fear you, and that will make you a far better parent than the ones you had to endure while you were growing up!

5. Let go of always needing to be right

One of the most common signs of an emotionally immature parent is the insatiable need to always be right. It's bad enough when you see two grown people arguing for the sake of proving one person right and the other person wrong. However, when it is an adult arguing with a child, the situation is beyond insane. Who in their right mind would need to prove their point to a five-year-old child anyway?! The chances are you know at least one person who fits that mold all too well. That said, in order to take yet another step away from becoming like your parents, it is vital that you recognize and eliminate any inherent need to always be right. The bottom line is that it is OK to be wrong. What isn't OK is to deny being wrong even when you know you are.

However, if you want to take this to the next level, you have to learn to avoid arguing your point even when you are right. After all, the problem isn't just in needing to always be right. The real problem is in needing to be right at someone else's expense. This is especially true when that other person is your child. It's fine if you and your child don't see eye to eye on a situation. In fact, it should be expected. You have had a lifetime of experiences and lessons that have given you the perspective you have. Your child, by contrast, has not. Therefore, you should never expect your child to be as wise as you. That is nothing more than a sign of emotional immaturity. Instead, accept that your child won't see things the way you do and allow them the space they need to learn the lessons their life has to teach them. Eventually, time will tell who is right and who is wrong on any particular issue. The important thing is to never compete with your child. This only makes them feel bad about themselves, and it makes you look like a monster, one that grows stronger by making your child weaker.

If you really want to have the ultimate experience, you can always join your child on their journey of discovery. Sure, your life has taught you plenty of lessons, but that doesn't mean that your child's life can't teach you even more. In fact, if you take the time to see life through your child's eyes, there's no telling what you might discover. Therefore, in those instances, when right and wrong really doesn't matter, take the time to see things through the eyes of your child. This will give you a fresh perspective on life, one that might open your mind to a whole new world full of wonder and excitement. At the very least, it will give you a chance to bond with your child on a whole new level, thus ensuring that they have a relationship with you that you never had with your parents. Even better, by looking at life through your child's eyes, you can begin to live the childhood you never had. Now you can play in the dirt and not have to worry about getting yelled at by the mean adults!

CHAPTER 11

Don't Give Up

While reading this book, you may have noticed just how challenging the self-healing process can actually be. For one thing, there is no magic wand that you can wave around and make the influences of the past miraculously disappear. Instead, you have to engage in numerous activities on a regular basis in order to free yourself from the hold your parents have on you even to this day. Additionally, some of the practices you have to engage in are highly disturbing. They bring you face to face with your inner demons and force you to fight them for your very life. During such an intense and demanding process, it is natural for even the strongest of people to want to give up and walk away in order to not have to deal with their past traumas anymore.

Unfortunately, this simply isn't an option. When you give up on the self-healing process, you only give in to the influences that your emotionally immature parents still have on you. Therefore, it is absolutely vital that you keep moving forward in the process, no matter how difficult, dark or disturbing it may become. The simple truth is that the harder the journey the greater the reward. Therefore, it is important that you remind yourself that only by overcoming your past can you begin to live the life you well and truly deserve. This chapter will discuss a few tips on how to keep going, even when you want to quit the most. By implementing these techniques into your self-healing process you will give yourself the best chance of success possible, and thus the best chance for finding happiness and wellbeing like never before!

Healing takes time

Perhaps the most important tip regarding self-healing is that of giving yourself the time you need. All too often, people expect instant results in whatever they do, self-healing included. In a society where everything is instant and convenient, it is no wonder that most people lack the willpower to see any long-lasting goal through to the end. However, when the stakes are as high as these, it is vital that you stay the course all the way to the proverbial finish line. Therefore, it is absolutely vital that you eliminate the mindset that expects instant results and replace it with one that is patient and enduring. Only then can you make the progress you need in order to live the life you desire.

A good technique for achieving this goal is to set reasonable goals. Thus, rather than having an "all or nothing" mindset break down your overall goal into smaller, more measurable goals. For example, you might give yourself a few weeks to integrate yoga into your daily routine, or you might set yourself a goal of practicing meditation every day by the end of the month. Each step forward will take you closer to your overall goal. Therefore all that matters is that you keep taking those steps, one at a time, and let everything else take care of itself. Don't expect instant results, and don't give up on yourself when you aren't as far along as you want. As long as you keep putting the time and effort into the process, it will produce the results you both desire and deserve.

Keep track of your progress

Another good way to deal with the length of the self-healing process is to keep track of your progress. Again, when you only pay attention to the finish line, it can seem as though the race will never end. However, when you take the time to record your progress, focusing on even the smallest of wins, you begin to feel a sense of accomplishment even though the finish line is still a long way off. The bottom line is that as long as you continue to put in the time and effort, you will make progress. Therefore, recognize the progress you are making and give yourself the credit and appreciation you deserve. This process is not one to be taken lightly. Therefore every step you take to achieving your self-healing goal is a victory in and of itself. Learn to celebrate these victories and to find joy in the journey.

Perhaps the best way to truly measure your progress is to keep a list of the things that would trigger your parents into becoming their worst. Start to record how you react to those situations each and every time you are faced with them. Eventually, you will see your behavior evolve, resulting in you seeming less and less like your parents with each experience. When you see yourself moving away from the influence of your parents, you know you are going in the right direction. Once you start seeing the results, it won't matter how long the process takes. You know you are improving each and every day, and that's all that really counts. In fact, the more time you spend is, the better you will become, so the longer the process, the better!

Hold yourself accountable

Sometimes it can be all too tempting to take time off of a demanding recovery process, especially one that requires as much soul searching and demon-fighting as recovering from emotionally immature parents. The problem with this is that if you take time off, it becomes harder to get back into the routine, and thus you begin to lose not only your momentum but you begin to lose the ground you have already gained. In order to prevent this from happening, it is vital that you hold yourself accountable.

One way to hold yourself accountable is to practice the previous method of setting goals. When you set regular, measurable goals, you ensure that you maintain a certain momentum that will take you closer and closer to your goal. Writing down those goals is a sure way to stay motivated as the last thing you want is to have your failed goals staring you in the face each and every day, making you feel defeated.

Holding yourself accountable may require more discipline than you have, and that isn't uncommon. In the event that you find yourself falling behind despite your best efforts, you may want to bring in other people. When you hold yourself accountable to others, you remove the ability to ignore the times you fail to put in the time and effort needed to make progress. Therefore, if you can't manage your efforts alone ask someone else to help you. By sharing your goals and expectations with others, you give yourself added motivation to stay on track. As bad as it is to let yourself down, it is even worse to admit failure to someone else. Not wanting to look bad in front of others can make all the difference between staying on track and letting yourself give up when the challenge becomes too hard.

Find someone you can confide in

Another benefit to sharing your goals and expectations with another person is the prospect of finding someone you can confide in. There will be times along your journey when you need to talk to someone you can trust. Whether you need to blow off some steam, reveal your fears, discuss your struggles or just find a shoulder to cry on, having someone there can be one of the most important elements of your self-recovery process. Such a person can give you the energy and support you need to push through even the toughest of times, thereby keeping you on track no matter how hard the journey becomes. Furthermore, they can celebrate your wins with you, cheering you on from one win to the next. Anyone who has ever accomplished anything worthwhile has always said they could never have done it alone. Instead, they credit their success to the love and support of those around them. If you want to give yourself the best chance of success, you should follow their lead and not try to accomplish the self-healing process alone.

Turn your losses into gains

Every process comes with its share of wins and losses, successes, and failures. The difference between those who succeed and those who fail comes down to one simple trick. Always turn your losses into gains. No one can avoid every pitfall and setback on their path to success, so there is no use in even trying. Instead, accept the setbacks as they come and become a better person for them. This is the trick of winning even when you suffer a defeat.

One way to achieve this is to get back up after every setback and get back in the race. This simple act will redefine the very nature of setbacks. Many see failure as the end of the journey. Thus they fear it with every step they take. Alternatively, successful people see failure as a chance to prove themselves. By getting up after a setback and resuming your course, you prove that you are stronger than the setbacks you face. This will remove the fear of failure from your mind and thus make you a stronger person as a result.

Another way to turn losses into gains is to recognize that every failure is, in fact, a learning opportunity. Most inventions went through countless prototype phases before the final version was designed. Rather than treating a prototype that didn't work as a failure, inventors learned the lessons from the experience and used their newfound knowledge to create a better design, one that would eventually work and bring them success. Therefore, see each and every setback as a chance to learn valuable lessons, ones that make you smarter, stronger, and better all around. When you view failure in this way, even your greatest failure becomes something of value, something that leads to your eventual and total success.

Once you achieve the mindset of turning losses into gains, you can begin to change the way your past affects your present life. Now, rather than being ashamed and angry about your childhood, you can see your childhood as a valuable source of experience, knowledge, and opportunity. The example set by your emotionally immature parents can be the thing that makes you the best parent imaginable. Furthermore, the pain and suffering you experienced as a child can be the thing that ensures you provide your children with the love, happiness, and security they deserve. In the end, you may have lost your childhood, but it doesn't mean you have lost your life overall. Instead, you have a wonderful life ahead of you, one in which you are free to be your best self, free to be the best friend, spouse, and parent anyone could hope for. Therefore, you can take your lost childhood and turn it into the best marriage for your partner, or the best childhood for your own children. This is the ultimate way in which you can turn your losses into gains!

CONCLUSION

Now that you have read this book, you have everything you need to reclaim your life and become the person you desire to be. No matter how toxic or traumatic your childhood may have been, you can now begin the process of self-healing, and thus rid yourself of the pain and suffering that has plagued you for your whole life. Even if the road to recovery is long, at least you know that you are going in the right direction and that happiness is within reach. With each and every step you take down the road to recovery, you will feel happier, healthier, and freer than ever before. Here are some key points to remember as you embark on your self-healing process:

- By understanding your parents, you can better understand the negative impact they have had on you.

- By recognizing your own struggles, you can begin to overcome them with the right self-healing techniques.

- As you practice self-care and other self-healing methods, you will begin to transform your life from one of trauma to one of triumph.

- The important thing is to always be honest and true to yourself.

- You *can* undo the effects of your toxic past and become the person you want to be.

- Once you take control of your life, there is *nothing* you can't do.

You might find the road to recovery to be fairly short and straight forward. Alternatively, you might find it to be a long road that will test your willpower and resolve, pushing you to your limits time and again. The important thing to remember is that the harder the journey, the bigger the prize. Each and every step forward is a step away from your past and one closer to your future, a future full of love, happiness, and a healthy sense of self-worth. Once you heal the wounds of your past, you will be able to be the friend, companion, and parent that people would do anything to have. Just remember, no matter how hard the journey may be, you are worth the effort. You deserve to have a happy and satisfying life, one that uncovers and fulfills your true potential!

As a final note, thank you for reading this book. If you have gained the insights and direction you need to turn your life around, please take the time to leave a review so that others can be made aware of this book and the benefits it has to offer. Again, thank you for reading this book, and the very best of luck to you on your road to self-healing and the happy life you truly deserve!

Sources

http://www.grandtimes.com/Creative_Visualization.html

http://www.heartspiritmind.com/relationships/relationships-with-emotionally-immature-people/

https://greatist.com/live/divorcing-parent#4

https://thriveglobal.com/stories/7-signs-you-re-in-a-toxic-relationship/

https://tinybuddha.com/blog/how-to-leave-a-toxic-relationship-when-youre-still-in-love/

https://www.bustle.com/p/11-signs-your-partner-is-emotionally-immature-61048

https://www.heysigmund.com/toxic-relationship-15-signs/

https://www.huffpost.com/entry/20-selfcare-practices-for_b_10314820

https://www.huffpost.com/entry/parents-who-drive-you-cra_b_7511242

https://www.medicalnewstoday.com/articles/320392.php

https://www.ncbi.nlm.nih.gov/pmc/articles/PMC3584580/

https://www.sfwomenstherapy.com/relationships/emotionally-immature-parents/

https://www.verywellmind.com/what-is-cognitive-behavior-therapy-2795747

https://www.vivianmcgrath.com/emotionally-immature-parents/

https://www.vivianmcgrath.com/emotionally-immature-parents-how-to-heal/

https://www.wikihow.com/Overcome-Emotional-Immaturity

Made in the USA
Middletown, DE
06 May 2021